Time Study

Blandford Management Series
General Editor: Geoffrey J. Athill, MBE, FMS, MIAM, AMBIM

TRAINING
Michael Jinks

FINANCE
Dennis Parkinson

TIME STUDY
Tony A. Jay

Blandford Management Series

Time Study

Tony A. Jay

BLANDFORD PRESS
Poole   Dorset

First published in the U.K. 1981

Copyright © 1981 Blandford Press Ltd.
Link House, West Street,
Poole, Dorset, BH15 1LL

British Library Cataloguing in Publication Data

Jay, Tony A
  Time study. – (Blandford management series).
  1. Time study
  I. Title
  658.5'421   T60.4

ISBN 0 7137 1085 3 (Case)
     0 7137 1126 4 (Limp)

Set in 11/12pt V.I.P. Baskerville and Printed and bound by
Fakenham Press Limited, Fakenham, Norfolk.

Contents

Acknowledgements

The publishers are grateful to the following for permission to reproduce material: the *Daily Express*; the McGraw-Hill Book Company (UK) Limited; British Standards Institution, 2 Park Street, London W1A 2BS, from whom complete copies of B.S. 3138 1979 can be obtained.

Chapter One

Introduction to Time Study

Time study was first introduced in the USA as a major means of measuring, improving, and controlling work. Frederick Winslow Taylor developed this skill as we know it at the turn of the century. Taylor wrote several books on his works, including time study, and even today he is called 'The Father of Scientific Management'. At much the same period, but quite independently, Frank B. Gilbreth was developing similar concepts, but with the aid of cinephotography. Since that time, of course, much has been written about both skills, separately and in combination. The term 'time and motion study' is now quite familiar.

The study of time at work is of significant importance to all companies and organisations, and Taylor explored the preparation of time and its application very thoroughly. Today, we often think of time study and motion study from those early days as work study, or even management services; such are the changes of history.

Work study itself consists of two major divisions:

1   the study of method – method study;
2   the study of time – work measurement.

Within the scope of work measurement, we recognise as many as seven or eight different techniques, used for the measurement of work. One of these is known in Britain as time study, and it is upon this single technique that this book has been written. From the outset, then, the reader is asked not to confuse the time study of Taylor with time study as a work measurement technique.

In principle, little has changed in Taylor's time study since its inception, except that it has increased in depth, and the

1

terminology changed, as it has travelled the world. Today, in Britain, the work that Taylor did as basic stopwatch studies we now call time study, and his wider, more far-sighted views are added to those of Gilbreth and others, and called work study.

British Standard terminology is used throughout this book, and a start showing the layout of the terms is made here with the subject of the book: time study.

B.S. 3138 1979 TIME STUDY NO. 41001
A work measurement technique designed to establish the time for a qualified worker to carry out specified elements under specified conditions at a defined rate of working, recorded by direct observation of the times, using a time measuring device and the ratings for the individual elements.

Other Techniques

Work measurement in many respects is more sophisticated now than it has ever been, though it is not always used in the optimum manner. It includes techniques that will measure almost any aspect of work. The major techniques include pre-determined motion time systems (P.M.T.S.), synthesis, activity sampling, comparative estimating, and analytical estimating. Each has its own quite different characteristics, and optimum areas of application. When time study cannot cope, owing to the nature of the work being studied, one of the other techniques will almost certainly do the job.

The purpose of this book is to examine time study in isolation from the other techniques. It is probably still the most widely used means of measuring work in Britain, and a recent survey indicates its continuing popularity in the USA. The same cannot be said of other countries. For example, the Swedes are rather more interested in the use of pre-determined motion time systems. The continuing use of time study in some areas can be attributed to tradition, but a second major factor could well be a lack of understanding about work measurement on the part of the employers. It seems that once a technique is adopted, be it time study, P.M.T.S. or sampling, there is reluctance on the part of management to expand that base.

2

Economic Implications

An interesting consideration that should be made at this early stage concerns the potential economic implications.

1   There are approximately 26 million people at work in Britain.

2   At an annual labour cost of say £5,000 per annum, per person, the cost of employing the nation's labour force is over £130,000,000,000 per annum.

3   By employing the labour force just 1% more effectively, we could either: a) save £1,300,000,000 per annum; b) produce 1% more for the same cost; or c) release 260,000 people in increased holidays or early retirement.

Many will see this as an over-simplification, but there would without doubt be significant economic advantage to the nation if this 1% improvement could be achieved.

An extract from the *Daily Express* in 1977 contradicts the above figures, but suggests an even wider significance. This is shown in fig. 1.

Some would say, and rightly, that not everyone is measured with a stopwatch; indeed no one knows how many are. The fact remains, however, that a significant number are measured by the watch, and therefore a cost of economic significance is implied.

Quality of Time Study

So far, reference has only been made to the effects of a 1% improvement. Several studies have shown, including research by universities, that the error in time study based schemes can be as wide as ± 20%. This is truly a reflection of poor application, and is not an inherent failure of the technique. Not unnaturally, when things go so sadly wrong, the temptation is to blame the technique rather than the management. Indeed, as knowledge of the technique is relatively poorly recorded in our libraries, it is difficult to blame the managers. Hence, for the moment, the problem continues to exist.

Pressure from the unions and the attitudes of management, giving usually the benefit of the doubt, ensure that errors in

The magic 1 per cent

'400,000 could be in work'

By Barrie Devney

DOLE queues could be slashed by a staggering 400,000 if Britain could increase its share of world trade—by only one per cent.

And a five per cent cut in imported manufactured goods would create work for a further 150,000 on the dole.

These glittering possibilities for a brighter future were presented yesterday by the Confederation of British Industry.

They came when the C.B.I., whose members employ more than 10 million workers launched a short, but challenging battle plan to achieve a more prosperous Britain.

It follows unprecedented consultations by C.B.I. leaders with 2,000 businessmen, cabinet ministers headed by Prime Minister Mr. James Callaghan, and the unions.

Taxes

Introducing the plan — "Programme for Action '77 ?" —C.B.I. president Lord Watkinson, said : "This is the platform from which the C.B.I. and its members will fight."

It insists on LESS inflation, government interference in industry, and taxes; MORE trade, jobs, incentives, involvement, and efficiency, and BETTER marketing.

The C.B.I.'s document proclaims boldly : " The opportunity is there; we owe it to ourselves and our country to succeed."

The aim of the five-point action programme is to create a million productive jobs over the next 18 months in an economy revitalised by competition and the restoration of real rewards for enterprise and effort.

To achieve the objective, the C.B.I. calls for :—

1 Inflation to be cut to an annual rate of five per cent, by mid-1978.

2 Public spending to be axed by £3,000 million 1979-80 so that resources are switched to production.

3 Pay Policy to be adjusted so that wages do not stoke up inflation but in a way that guarantees proper rewards for initiative, skill and responsibility at all leves of industry.

Saving

4 Invovement of all sections of industry in efforts to step up productivity and efficiency so that company profitability is rebuilt, and import-saving can be achieved.

5 Greater efforts by Government, managements and unions to ensure that manufacturing companies become more competitive and make the gains in world markets which the C.B.I. believes are not only essential but possible.

Speaking at a meeting of South East business men in London yesterday Lord Watkinson stressed that the success of the C.B.I.'s plan would depend to a great extent on Government willingness to slash the tax burden.

● The latest out of work figures for December stood at 1,370,000.

Fig. 1   Article appearing in the Daily Express *on 7 January 1977.*

4

issued times are rarely minus. Standard times in this country will in fact almost always vary from 0 to 20% *too generous at the time of issue*. In a short space of time after issue, many of these 'standards' will only show the position at the time of issue. Methods, conditions, equipment change, usually for the better, and the 'standards' rapidly become theoretically obsolete. This does not mean that the times will be rendered obsolete by management. They will under normal circumstances continue to be used, and in time become a major factor in wages drift. Aubrey Jones, in his work at the National Board for Prices and Incomes, spent some time on this feature of the economy, and made special mention of incentive schemes as a major cause of wages drift and hence inflation. Time study is usually the basis of those same incentive schemes. It is much too easy to infer from this that the cause is time study, or incentives. This is far from the truth. It is the quality of application that is at fault, and thus by inference the quality of management. We may choose, as a society, to carry on with our heads in the sand, blaming the technique, or we can begin to ask ourselves if there is perhaps another simple reason. If we employ a quack doctor for cheapness, can we assume, at his failure, that the medical profession is a failure? Indeed, would we blame the quack doctor? Is it not even conceivable that the fault is our own?

In the manufacturing industries, where time study is most widely used, it will be practised in the production departments, which employ the largest section of the labour force. These are also the sections which have the most significant trade union representation.

Clearly then, we are dealing with a subject of considerable importance, even if it is not the most popular of the 'arts'.

The Hidden Cost

The data produced from time study has many valuable uses for management, and is increasingly becoming computerised as cost data, planning data and training data. Each company that uses it should be deeply aware, not only of the initial advantages, but also of the implications of using it in a slipshod manner.

One comparison that could be used to illustrate this is the spraying of an older car. We could just lightly sand over the rusting parts, and then complete with an attractive top spray. For a short while there will be an improvement, with which one could be very pleased. Soon, however, the hidden rust will begin to spread and reappear on the surface, and we shall be really quite disappointed.

How many organisations in this country have incentive schemes with similar characteristics? Rather more than our managers would believe or admit.

As an alternative, we could have replaced the rusting areas by welding in new metal, prior to spraying. The cost is slightly greater, but the life of the car much enhanced.

The same philosophy can be applied to incentive schemes based on standard times. It will cost a little more to do it well, but it is worth it in the long run.

Interdependence of Time Study with Other Techniques

As already stated, the purpose of this book is to explore the significance, indeed the art, of time study as an independent subject. This is possible in a theoretical work, though in practice it can never be applied as a totally independent technique. There are a number of other techniques and concepts with which it is inevitably and rightly associated. Throughout the text, therefore, reference is made to those other techniques and concepts. This will, I hope, put the particular aspect under discussion into sharper perspective.

The Practitioner

If we start from the simple point that someone, somewhere, is actually employed to apply the technique, then the question is – where might this person be found?

Time study is really one of the techniques deeply embedded in the field of work study. Indeed there are still many people who look upon time study and work study as the same thing; perhaps this is a throwback to the days of Taylor. A more precise picture is given in fig. 2, with an even greater expansion of work measurement shown in fig. 3.

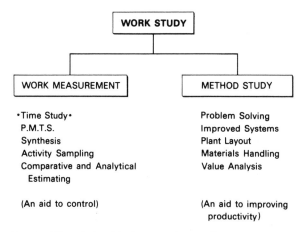

Fig. 2   The relationship between time study and work study.

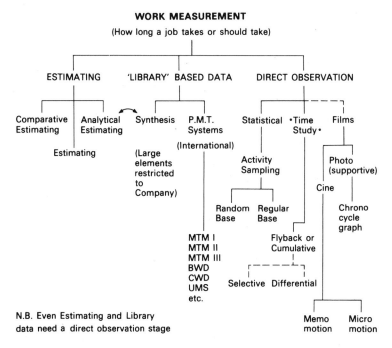

Fig. 3   A further analysis of professional work measurement techniques.

Work Study and Management Services

Work study has two further involvements in its own right.

1   Work study to many is not only synonymous with time study but also with incentive schemes. Hence, if you have work study you have incentive schemes, and if you have incentive schemes you have time study. There are exceptions, of course, but this is often the rule.

2   Work study in the larger organisations is often only one section of a larger management services unit. This department might be called productivity services, or even industrial engineering, the name used in the USA.

This larger department may well include such sections as:

organisation & methods;   value analysis;
internal consultancy;   operational research;
systems analysis;   production engineering;

and indeed even the computer and cost accounts. Everything depends upon the nature of the business, and the company philosophy and structure.

Time study as a technique, therefore, is normally carried out by:

management services officers; work study officers;
O & M practitioners;   time study officers.

Someone applying time study, then, could either be quite a junior in the department or in some cases a very senior officer, capable in time of becoming the Managing Director. Naturally the quality and result of work done could be vastly different. Everything depends upon whom you employ, your own knowledge of the art, and the potential value it offers. The company philosophy, or policy, will develop according to the managers, yet experience to date indicates that not enough is understood about this subject. The best techniques are based on solid foundations. Many managers have strong *views* on work study, and probably the majority *suffer* the techniques. Yet practised at its optimum, work study is a fine, valuable and fascinating profession.

The Application

It is well enough known that work measurement data is used as an aid to *control*. Time study, the subject of this book, is one of the most widely practised work measurement techniques perhaps in the world, and certainly in Britain. A major consideration, and a fundamental one, is how the data is used.

Much has already been written on the subject over the years, but probably not as much as it deserves. Consider for a moment how important any basic information is to a company. Information is often the very lifeblood of the whole enterprise. Stop the flow of information, and the organisation itself will cease to function.

Consider further the quality and reliability of the work measurement data. It is used in payment systems, planning output, pricing, training, much of it the basis of computer analysis – *but what if the data is incorrect?*

One well-known saying amongst business people concerning the computer is 'Garbage in – garbage out'. A computer can only be as good as the data it receives. This means quite simply that if you put in the wrong data, or use an inadequate programme, the output data will be incorrect or relatively weak. The same principle applies exactly to any company.

If the company uses poor methods, and measures those methods, then the resultant 'control' is the control of a poor system. If also the company measures those jobs in a hurry, using relatively inexperienced staff, it is not really considering the true economics of the situation. Subsequently the times issued will tend to be generous, and the viability of the company that much the poorer. To have sent someone on a three-week measurement course is not enough. To employ someone who has just qualified is not enough. Experience, judgement and developed ability are also necessary.

Assuming that you use incentive schemes, or are about to do so, remember that the economics of the situation only start with labour cost. The cost of plant, space and power will ultimately be included. You may be using all these items of cost very effectively, or even very ineffectively, without actually knowing

9

how truly effective you are. One fact that is inescapable is that in using time study as a means of work measurement you are delegating the responsibility for establishing many of those costs to a work study department. It is the easiest thing in the world for your computer, your accountants, your planners or trainers to accept whatever the work study department produces, but it is the managers who are going to be ultimately responsible for the results. Regretfully, for a whole list of reasons, often management-sponsored in ignorance, the resultant data is not always as sound as it might be. If you give a junior work study officer a week to complete a job that is best done in a month by a senior work study officer, who are you to blame when it goes wrong?

Like a computer, *a company is only as good as the data upon which it is based!*

How can Management Judge its Own Ability?

Clearly, in saying this, there are other implications not to be ignored. The company philosophy, the human relations, and many other factors are absolutely vital. The point being made is that if a company establishes that the cost of a product should be £500, and in its manufacture it proves reasonable, with product cost varying between £480 and £520, this is not necessarily good management.

Consider the possibility that, even at £500, there may still be relatively low wages, poor industrial relations, varying quality, and minimum control over production. Providing in the first instance that the company plans to manufacture at £500, and achieves this target, there must be some cause for satisfaction. If, on top of this, the company sells those products and makes a profit, they may rightly claim some success.

Assume next that a competitor begins to produce a similar product. The cost of this new product is £450, wages are higher, industrial relations are better, and quality and production are under tight control. Clearly the competitor has better managers; but how does the first company *know*, until a better product, not only cheaper but of a similar or superior quality, is produced? *Is it really unreasonable to compare Britain with say*

Germany or Japan? In the case of the first company, producing at
£500, making a fair profit with a moderately happy labour force
and some public prestige all prove that the business is successful, but how long will it last? Amongst other products, it could
be said of some British companies that they met the above
criteria at one time. They used to manufacture motor-cycles
and typewriters.

One secret of good business, surely, is to be so good that it is
hardly worthwhile for another company to try and compete in
that market. The 'cost plus' approach to business will only
work as long as no one else spots a market with a high cost base,
or where it is subsidised.

The Level of Practitioner

A major consideration in the quality of time study is the effect
caused by the size of the company.

Let us start with the exaggerated situation of the company
large enough to need, as they see it, one work study officer only.
He will inevitably work almost alone, rather than as a member
of specific but natural group of staff. Nevertheless he must
report to someone, perhaps the works manager. His position in
the organisational structure depends upon having to put him
somewhere.

1 How high should he be placed?
2 How much should he be paid?
3 What scope and responsibility should he be given?

This early and vital decision must reflect the skills he needs to
perform his duties at an optimum level for the company. Offer a
vacancy at say £10,000 per annum, reporting directly to the
Board of Directors, and demanding a high degree of proven
skill, and you will get a certain kind of professional. Change
your mind, and offer £5,500 per annum, reporting to the works
manager, and requiring just one year's experience, and you will
have a different type of person applying. The final financial and
other benefits that will be achieved will be as different as the
two job descriptions imply. The decision is a management one,
and the results a management responsibility.

11

It is probably fair to say that a company which employs only one work study officer also employs a small number of managers in production, again perhaps only one. The work study officer will have to be given a lower salary and status! He will thus be relatively young and inexperienced, and will probably spend most of his time on the measurement of work for incentive schemes. As this is likely to be his main function, 'and almost anyone can be trained for this work', it is inevitable that his work will not be performed as effectively as it might be. This means that the work of the employees will not be performed as effectively as it might be, and this could prove to be a costly and ill-advised decision. In the larger company, there may be a very experienced work study manager for the junior members to turn to for advice, and who will in any event ensure that the work is of a high standard. There is a distinct possibility, then, that the smaller company may be turning its back, through lack of knowledge and advice, on the full potential of management services and work study. In time, this situation will become consolidated; everyone who experiences the service given reaches their own conclusions about 'time and motion study', *and they are so often wrong.*

In such a company, the type of work study practitioner attracted to any future vacancies, limited by salary offered alone, will inevitably also be young, inexperienced, narrow in opportunity, ability and effect. He will lack the skills and confidence needed to correct the imbalance, and the bad reputation of time and motion study, though unsoundly based, will become ever more deeply entrenched.

Yet, even in such a case, the practitioner could quite conceivably have it within his 'power' to affect the wages cost, potential production output, industrial relations and even profits far beyond the cost of employing him. Thousands of managers and accountants in this country are quite happy to accept the figures he prepares, no matter how poor they may be; after all it is not their responsibility. There is an overwhelming case for demanding higher standards, but few people do so as it is not their responsibility.

You can ask your own work study officer or manager if, in his view:

1   work study is being used *fully professionally*;
2   it is achieving all that it might.

You do not, of course, have to believe the answers, but it is very easy to predict with confidence what they will be. It is even quite easy to predict how the manager will react. He will probably not even be prepared to put the questions either to himself or to his work study department.

An Evaluation

Take for example the measuring of a small section employing five people, or 5 × 40 hours/week × 48 weeks/year at £2.00/hour. Objective is a bonus scheme. Dependent upon the complexity of the work, this could take say one month. Standard times might be issued, dependent upon the skill of the measurer, at 5%, 10%, 15% or *even 30% too generous*. The less experienced the work study officer, the more likely he is to be wrong. In this example, there is no one he can turn to for advice, support or confirmation. He is more than likely under pressure from the manager, the accountant or trade unions to issue the times quickly, and is tempted to submit. It is his responsibility, but at this stage no one can say he is wrong. He thus issues the times, either believing or hoping that all is well.

In order to make a calculation, let us accept the common figure of looseness at 10%, but that a useful reduction in hours is made. The total man hours suggested are reduced from 200 hours per week to 132. Because they are 10% loose, the hours *should have been 120*. Fig. 4 shows a calculated example.

Now in this calculation we have considered the effects of employing a junior work study officer *for one month only*. He could well produce the same kind of diminished benefit every month in which he is employed, and still be congratulated. The reason is that at the time no one is aware that the standard times are 10% too generous. Of course, in three or four months' time, when the operators are earning above the predicted levels, everyone will say it is because they are working so well – a further reason for self-congratulation within the management team. Where, oh where, did wisdom go?

Refer back to fig. 1, and consider once more the magic 1%.

a) Present Labour Cost   = 200 × 48 × £2·00   = £19,200 pa

b) Proposed Labour Cost = 132 × 48 × £2·00
                              + bonus at 0·67   = £16,917 pa

         A successful project saving   = £ 2,283 pa

Yet because the times were unprofessionally
generous, the proposed labour cost
should have been   c)   = 120 × 48 × £2·67   = £15,379 pa

      A more successful project saving   = £ 3,821 pa

       This gives an *additional saving* of   £ 1,538 pa

Fig. 4   The lost benefits that many companies may suffer on one project.

It is the continuation of these unnecessary gifts that is the rust, hidden by a thin layer of paint, that helps to weaken our economy (an economy that could be as strong as that of Japan). Using a more experienced practitioner would have cost more money in two ways. Firstly he would have had to be paid a higher salary, and secondly he would have taken longer. Let us say the cost of a junior for one month would be £400, and the cost of a senior for six weeks would be £800. Nevertheless, using a more experienced practitioner would have yielded even greater benefits. This is not an assumption but a fact.

The financial benefits from one project over a five-year period, comparing the two levels of experience, are shown in fig. 5.

	Using Junior W.S.O.			Using Senior W.S.O.		
	Cost	Benefit	Balance	Cost	Benefit	Balance
Year one	£ 400	£ 2,283	£ 1,883	£ 800	£ 3,821	£ 3,021
Year two	–	£ 2,283	£ 4,166	–	£ 3,821	£ 6,842
Year three	–	£ 2,283	£ 6,449	–	£ 3,821	£10,663
Year four	–	£ 2,283	£ 8,732	–	£ 3,821	£14,484
Year five	–	£ 2,283	£11,015	–	£ 3,821	£18,305

This accumulation is repeated over and over again each time a project is completed.

Fig. 5   The accumulative effect of lost benefit, again from one project.

Although the accumulative effect of one poor work study officer is apparently good for profit, *it is still well below what might have been*. There are few companies in this country which are prepared to have such calculations made; one can only assume that they are unable to believe the extent of possible benefits. There can be no logic in being aware of these facts and continuing to accept lower standards than are achievable. On the other hand, it is so easy to blame the unions.

The following extract is taken from the latest edition of *Maynard's *Industrial Engineering Handbook*:

> The problems of costs and standards and human relations should be apparent to all; but increasingly there has been a tendency, among those who are not directly involved in the problem, to be carried away by the mystique of automation and cybernation and to conclude that work study is an obsolescent technique.
>
> Such a conclusion obscures the hard fact that a time standard – whether of machine time or man time, and *whether precise or not* – is essential in the control of production, the synthesis of cost, the payment of wages, and the projection of manufacturing budgets. Time Study is the medium whereby technological gains are quantified and consolidated.

* This book is recognised throughout the world as being one of the finest books, if not the finest, on this vital subject. The three major objectives of industrial engineering are:

1 to improve productivity (and thus profit);
2 to improve management control;
3 to improve industrial relations.

In a modern competitive world such as ours, these objectives are only too clearly of major economic significance.

Chapter Two

Implications for Industrial Relations

The most important feature about time study is the esteem in which it is held. For most people, this is a negative feeling rather than a positive one. Mention work study or management services to some and they may not be sure at first to what you refer. A brief discussion, mention the *stopwatch*, and the reaction is immediate: 'Oh, you mean time and motion study?' This is a common reaction from the young, even though the name 'time and motion study' stopped being used officially before they were born. At least, it still seems to have some mystique and reputation. In the USA it is the reverse.

Regrettably, the reputation developed to a large extent at the time of the depression, and is more frequently bad than good. The question is – to what extent is that reputation deserved?

Reluctance to be Studied

In addition to this, however, we have the very powerful psychological aspect of one person standing alongside another, at their place of work, and making detailed observations of time. No holds barred, the time study officer wishes to know every minute detail of what the operator is doing, and why. At the same time he (or she) will be clicking that infernal button on the watch, and recording the time everything takes.

From an entirely human point of view, this cannot and will not ever be popular. It is natural that the operator is concerned, and will want to ask questions: Why select me? How long will it take? Is it really necessary? and many more.

Reluctance to Take a Study

Consider for a moment the feelings of someone taking a time study. The thought of standing and observing someone else at work is very rarely popular, in its own way it is almost as unpopular to have to take a study as it is to be studied. Naturally one does become used to it. Nevertheless, work study officers, in the main, much prefer to sit in their offices and do calculations, attend meetings, write reports, or undertake method study.

Opportunity to Learn

The problem is that unless the work study officer becomes very familiar with the job, probing into its very depths, then it is impertinent to attempt to tell employees and management how long the job should take.

What finer way is there, apart from acquiring the actual skill, to understand a job than by mentally absorbing every action, every skill, every problem, indeed the very nature of the job itself? There really are only two ways of understanding a job: skill in the hands and skill in the mind. And here we have two quite different understandings, both of considerable advantage to any management.

This mental understanding of the nature of work is not available to many people, and it really ought to be. One outstanding example is that of the production engineer: he understands in great depth the technical aspects of the work for which he is responsible, and then delegates the acquiring of knowledge of the human content to time study officers. They do this because they do not like taking time studies themselves. It is a poor excuse to suggest that the work is below their level of ability. The study of human beings at work can in many cases be even more complex than metals cutting.

Executive Consideration

Senior executives should take careful note of this delegation of responsibility. The question should be asked as to whether it is

17

in the interest of the company or in the interest of the production engineer. There is a small percentage of production engineers who would absolutely agree with the advantages of studying *all* work. Some have even expressed amazement at what can be achieved as they become converted. Take a small case history for example. An operator of a machine was asked by a time study officer if it could be run any faster. 'Oh yes', replied the operator, 'but the production engineer has laid down these feeds and speeds.' The production engineer was invited to join the discussion. Within an hour, it was agreed to make adjustments that led to an increase in output of over 30%. The operator was quite happy in this instance to do the extra. The production engineer said he had not had time to revise the feeds and speeds to keep up with the changing technology. In many cases it is *getting to know the machine operators* on closer terms that allows such co-operation. How is this relationship to develop if the production engineer sends out a time study officer with often only two or three weeks' training in the use of a stopwatch to take the studies?

The Reaction of Industry

The norm in industry then, is as follows.

The work study officer does not really want to take studies. The operator does not really want to be studied. The managers and supervisors do not really want the fellow with the stopwatch in their department. The trade unions are not exactly keen to have studies done, but do accept their use in many cases.

One needs to establish quite clearly then whether the data produced by the watch is really needed at all. One must also consider alternative means.

Alternatives

There seems little doubt that the data produced is of considerable value. It is also true that there are a number of alternative means of producing it. With technology, designs and methods in an almost constant state of change, there seems to be no real alternative to direct observation, i.e. to be there, to see, to understand, and to be fair. In the 1980s the need to update standard times will increase. This does not necessarily mean time study, but in many cases this is considered to be the optimum means of providing that data.

Change

Probability of change
In addition to the collection of data, and all the human implications, one is also faced with the circumstances involved in the use to which the data is put. In collecting data, one is either measuring change that has occurred, or one will use the data to bring about change. After all, if nothing has changed, or is desired to be changed, why waste money collecting data? *The ultimate objective of collecting data is to measure change, initiate change or to increase control.*

Logically, if the data collected is about certain jobs, and thus certain people, and is used for change, it will of course affect those people. For example:

method study – retraining in new method, or even new jobs;
incentives – change in the rate of working and the levels of earnings.

Resistance to change
One of the most popular fallacies in industry and commerce is that people are resistant to change. Essentially this is a widespread misunderstanding. Basically we all welcome change in principle, and accept it as a part of our lives. Natural instincts warn us, however, against change for change's sake. Also, and very naturally, we resist any change that will make things less pleasant, or worse than that which we already have. If we are unable to assess whether the change will be for better or worse, and we suspect that it is being brought about by someone else for their own benefit, we may feel that the change for us will be worse, so we resist.

Hence one could suggest that the fallacy of resistance to

change has grown up amongst those who try to cause someone to suffer a 'loss', in order that they might gain. It is a true optimist who expects co-operation from those about to suffer *as a result of co-operation*.

When a change must occur, let it be for the better, not only for the changer, but for those being changed, and then it will be welcomed rather than resisted.

When people are unable to decide whether a proposed change is better or worse, due to lack of communications, they will naturally be very cautious. After all, if the change is good for them, why have they not been given an outline of the benefits?

There is another well known saying from the same philosophy: *better the devil you know*.

Benefits of change

It is probably fair to say that the stopwatch is tolerated by operators because it is linked with incentive schemes, and by management because incentives are linked with lower costs. Properly applied work study is, however, more, much more, than this.

The successful route to change, then, is simply to design the change so that things will be better for everyone, rather than merely a sectional advantage. This entails evaluating the total benefits thoroughly, and the possible disadvantages, and then to arrange the benefits so that a reasonable share goes to everyone. The disadvantages are also shared. In this way, not only can management make an assessment of the benefits but the operators can too. Communications need to be clear and open to discussion. All can thus see the implications involved. It should not need to be stated that after any change has been introduced a review of the reality will be made. Operators make this review as well as managers. It is perhaps wiser if the operators are able to look back and see that the change was better than they had been led to believe.

Gaining acceptance of change

One successful change will lead to more ready acceptance of the next. One failure could lead to mistrust, and this sticks more strongly than one acceptance. Never wrap up change in cotton wool.

Let us return now more directly to the practical implications of change as related to time study applications. Experience shows that it is always best to have some sort of rules or guidelines. These will not guarantee that industrial relations will improve, but they will certainly help. The following approach may be used where time study is the basis for measurement in an incentive scheme.

Naturally, this procedure cannot overrule company policy, or areas of agreement that may already operate. It is intended as advice, or as a guide, where no system now exists, or as a basis of comparison with an established informal system. Generally speaking, the procedure will be equally valid for method study.

1 Establish, or work within, a framework of company policy that has been thoughtfully prepared and agreed. A long-term view must be the best approach and this must be with trade union support, where relevant.
2 Always discuss at some length, both formally and informally, the project before it commences. Involve as many people to be directly affected as one reasonably can. Be prepared not to commence if there appear to be some reservations.
3 Continue discussions primarily informally, though where necessary formally, throughout the project, and if useful after completion.
4 Study as long as it is necessary for the time study officer really to understand every aspect of the work, and to get to know the people involved. Four visits could well be considered a minimum, though some projects may take several months.
5 Thoroughly evaluate all aspects of the work, so that the results are soundly based, and you are able to discuss those aspects with implications of change, at subsequent discussions. This should include a knowledge of the advantages and disadvantages.
6 Advise the management where the benefits to the

21

employees are so insignificant that change would naturally be 'resisted', and thus any resistance can be understood, perhaps even allowed for.

7   Carefully design the scheme so that it should operate effectively, and offers clear benefits to those involved. The paperwork system here is often quite critical.
8   Implement the scheme, always being available to help with any unforeseen problems.
9   Maintain the scheme regularly *with the support of management*. In many cases this maintenance, or method study, will necessitate repeating stages 2–8 once again.

Who is Involved?

The range of people directly involved in these work measurement projects is fairly narrow, but an analysis soon shows that there are quite a number indirectly involved.

1   Directly involved: a) those operators to be actually studied, plus colleagues in the same immediate group; b) the manager and his supervisors; c) trade union representatives.
2   Indirectly involved: a) other employees in the department; b) inspectors or other service staff; c) wages and cost clerks; d) Planning Department; e) full-time union officials possibly.

Whereas a company can establish its own set rules, in a book like this it is only possible to offer general ideas.

Implications of this Involvement

The overriding factor must clearly be *change*. The measurement of work has some ultimate purpose(s). The normal immediate aim is to produce 'standard times', and it is inevitable that they will be used as a primary source of data, perhaps even with secondary uses. As stated in Chapter One, there are six fundamentally different ways in which work measurement or work measurement data may be used. Of these six uses, it is very likely that in five cases the direct operators will be involved, not only in the preparation but in the application. It is only in the case of *pricing* that no immediate implication is discernible for the operators.

Incentives

In the case of introducing an incentive scheme, the direct operators are going to have the basis of their earnings changed. No more will they be paid by the number of hours worked, and a single rate per hour, but part of the wage will be due to their personal or group contribution. Dependent upon the type of scheme, hourly earnings may vary from week to week. Furthermore, if the average level of effort throughout the manufacturing areas is significantly raised, would this not lead to *less* employees being required than before?

Cost control

In the case of costing, data is supplied to the accounts department for use in pricing. Having pre-determined what cost should be, it is only logical that management should aim to hold actual cost at predicted cost levels. This control is directly linked with incentives, and must extend right to the shop floor, where the majority of cost is incurred. Standard costing, budgetary control and marginal costing are all dependent on standard times.

Training

As far as training is concerned, and assuming that in the work measurement exercise method study is completed first to provide a sound base, it is necessary to train the employees to a higher standard than before. The more successful the method study and work measurement programme, the more precise the training method has to be.

Evaluation

The major purpose of evaluation in this context is to help persuade management that recommended changes are worthwhile. Hence, it is very likely that when evaluation takes place change will quickly follow. For the operators this means acquiring new habits and skills, perhaps even moving to a new environment, or working with new colleagues.

Planning
Finally, in the case of planning, perhaps the implications are not too strong. Nevertheless, it may well necessitate introducing new systems or paperwork or priorities, and there can be minor irritations introduced, as well as the benefits of greater order.

Interviews and Discussions with People Involved

Clearly, the people most directly involved or affected must receive priority in any discussions held. The discussion itself must be prepared and 'tailored' to fit the ultimate purpose for undertaking the exercise. Two examples are given below of widely differing situations with equally differing implications.

Case 1   There is a bottleneck in the fettling department. The manager has requested work study to assist in overcoming this single problem.

Case 2   The company is introducing a productivity agreement into the organisation, and this is the first department to have work study officers coming into the department.

In both cases, however, there is a certain amount of common ground. Both situations require that the following four 'groups' are represented.

1   The management.
2   The trade unions (where appropriate).
3   The operators.
4   The work study department.

In case 1 above, it is likely that discussions are limited to the following.

1   The departmental manager and supervision.
2   The appropriate shop steward(s).
3   The operators to be measured and affected.
4   The work study staff actually involved.

In the more important case 2 above, a whole series of preliminary discussions and negotiations to formulate and agree on the work to be done will already have been completed at Board level.

The first departmental meeting might involve:

1 senior executives, even Board members;
2 senior personnel staff;
3 departmental manager and supervisors;
4 national and or local full-time union officials;
5 departmental shop stewards;
6 all departmental operators;
7 the work study manager and section leader;
8 work study practitioners involved.

Not only would there be the independent preliminary meetings of management, but the unions and the operators will have held separate meetings.

Following the full departmental meetings there will, or should be, further meetings as felt necessary or requested by: management; unions; operators; or work study.

Seeking co-operation
There can be no logic in a company setting out to cause employees harm or discomfort. They are more concerned with running an effective organisation, be it in the private or public sector. Even so, they often do not give that little extra consideration that their employees need and deserve.

Union representatives, on the other hand, are more concerned about their members, and rightly so. Inevitably there are different views about how things are best done. Nevertheless, experience shows that in the vast majority of cases employees and their representatives are honest and fair. They believe that it is management that is being unreasonable.

Despite a large area of agreement in philosophical terms, there persists in Britain a 'them and us' situation. In the main, this is precipitated and maintained by management in different companies. No one is seeking complete equality, but sometimes the gap really is too wide. In many cases, this becomes the basis of deep-rooted mistrust. This is avoided in many countries, and is an unnecessary tragedy where it exists in Britain.

The fact is that usually even the Directors of a company are only employees, and the more the company is successful the more benefits there are to share. Whether you are a manager, operator, trade unionist, accountant, whatever 'side' you are on, all stand to gain most when the company is well run and secure. A company verging on bankruptcy is surely of no value to the employees, the employers, the investors, or the country. The beneficiaries then are our overseas competitors. *The aim should be willing co-operation by discussing why, how, when, and the implications – in fact by thorough communications.*

Work study practitioners above all people should thus be deeply interested in the welfare of all, and must never become 'company men'.

Despite the fact that the primary purpose of work study is to save money, it should still be concerned about good working conditions, high wages, security of employment, indeed the welfare of the employees. This requires mutual respect, flexibility, and an interest in job enrichment. In time this should lead to improved industrial relations, and an improved standard of living for all. In short, intelligence and integrity are essential qualities in the practice of work study and time study. The management and employees may not feel they currently have these qualities in their work study officers, and should thus demand this in the longer term. It is not only naïve but also bad management practice to employ a poor quality work study officer on time study.

Existing Relationships

It will be recognised that a very complex set of relationships already exists within any department (manufacturing is used as the main example). An attempt has been made to illustrate this in fig. 6.

This set of relationships is quite delicately balanced. Personalities will often play a significant role. In many cases, despite gradual development resulting in a very solid base, it is

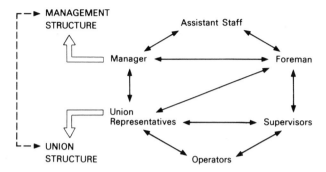

Fig. 6   A representation of communications within a department.

still susceptible to upset if circumstances or personalities change. The following are examples of such changes.

1 The start of a new manager.
2 A change of shop steward.
3 The introduction of numerically controlled machine tools requiring less staff.

Everyone in the department has a place, and a view. If the communications are good, and morale high, then there is a desire to leave things as they are. If change is being pressed for, then at least it could offer improvement. If morale is low at the outset, even then the employees may not see the possibility of improvement; they may indeed think that things could become even worse. Every effort to change for the better will be viewed with some suspicion.

Whatever the industrial or employee relations background, at least all in the department will know one another, and sense that relations are good, medium or poor. There will be a kind of solidarity even with the supervisors and manager. Inter-departmental relations will also exist, and are important.

Anyone not employed by or reporting directly to the manager will be an 'outsider'. Some outsiders will be more welcome than others, the tea lady being a good example. Each outsider should be aware of the image that their own particular department gives to them, and aim to improve that image by being

27

acceptable as a person and as an employee. This means much more than being liked; it also means doing one's job professionally, and gaining respect. To be respected is superior to being liked, in many senses.

The outsider, or visitor, can and frequently does alter the balance of departmental relationships. The work study officer, in particular, comes with his own 'time and motion' image. This is something that is better avoided or minimised. The nature of his work often means that he will stay for much longer periods than other visitors. Perhaps even a regular pattern of visits is necessary. His involvement is often deeper than other visitors, and could even become semi-permanent. Nevertheless, the work study officer will rarely report directly to the manager, though he will have direct access. The work study officer, then, would never be accepted as a true member of the department.

Possible New Relationships

During his visits to the department, a new set of relationships will inevitably develop. This need not be necessarily complicated, as there is a natural order of communications that should be understood and followed. The opportunity for informal communications, however, becomes apparent and can complement the formal channels. This is best understood by comparing figs. 6 and 7.

It is vital, therefore, that the visitors understand the balance of communications, and that the department understands the full implications of the work, and the reaction to work, of the visitors. There are thus two major objectives for the visitor.

1   To bring benefit to investors, management and employees.
2   To maintain, or even help to improve, industrial relations.

It is also necessary for the department to understand how the visitor works, and the complications of performing the work. For preference, management, visitors and employees should work as a team.

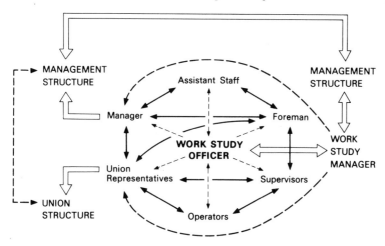

Fig. 7 The increase in number of channels of communication after the introduction of work study into a department.

Management Contribution to Industrial Relations

The contribution of management in the field of industrial relations, and indeed their responsibility, is clearly paramount. By management, here, one means all levels of management, and includes company objectives and policy. If relationships are good, management must take some of the credit. If, on the other hand, industrial relations are poor, management must take some of the blame. It is an unfair over-simplification to suggest that the fault lies with someone else.

If the company policy of any organisation includes an agreement to employ a work study department, then it is a prime responsibility of management to use work study in a way that enhances industrial relations. There are many examples in industry where management 'allow' work study to cause a decline in industrial relations. This is a failing of management, not a failing of work study. Fig. 8 shows how management policy must lie at the heart of industrial relations.

The only way management can use work study to enhance industrial relations is to understand how it is best used, and to

29

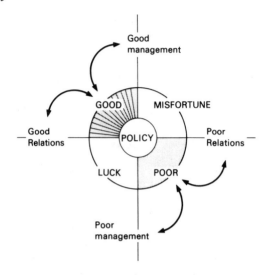

Fig. 8   The relationship between management policy and industrial relations.

ensure that it is practised at an optimum. This often only means ensuring that the members of the work study department are not only qualified but also thoroughly experienced.

Managers should recognise that introducing work study can change the normal channels of communication, and that this can be beneficial. Failure to recognise and use these changes can mean deterioration rather than gain.

Responsibility of Management Services

Management services and work study staff have a particular responsibility here. They should be aware of the implications of their role, as much as anyone. This is another reason for ensuring the right level of skill is employed. How can one expect young inexperienced practitioners to bear this burden? They may not even be aware of it, and even if they are they may not have the wisdom and maturity to cope with the situation. Many companies employ only young inexperienced practitioners, and maintain the *status quo* by limiting their activities and responsibilities. Perhaps in some cases the companies may have been wiser not to have introduced work study at all! Another ancient, yet valuable, saying is: *If you are going to do something, do it well, or don't do it at all!*

Responsibility for Issued Data

In completing his work, the work study officer may also be preparing a considerable amount of work that is not seen. Particular reference is made here to time study work. Documents such as the element description, set-up sheets and synthetic data will be described in later chapters. For some unexplainable reason, in many companies much of this information is retained solely by the work study department. It is not so much security, policy or logic as tradition or lack of understanding. Much of this 'retained' information could be of considerable interest and value to management and supervision, and should be issued to them, and used by them as a policy. It should not even be left to the discretion of management to use or not to use. Responsibility in its use should be strongly supported by an understanding of the benefits. If they are not provided with this data, and instructed in their responsibilities, they are unlikely to ask for it on a personal basis.

A very common complaint made by work study officers against managers is that they are not advised when changes take place. This makes the success of the incentive likely to collapse, due to lack of maintenance. The fact is that, because of lack of data and understanding, the managers often do not appreciate the basis, or reason, for advising changes to the department that issued the times. Given the understanding, the information and the responsibility, the manager will respond accordingly. Without these things, neither the manager nor the work study officer is to blame, but the system.

Who is responsible for the system?
Perhaps the fault does lie with work study practitioners. Simply because tradition suggests that certain data is restricted, they

follow the normal pattern. In introducing work study to a company, the management usually rely on the work study manager or consultant to advise on the system. In reality, however, there is no system recorded in books, or accepted by the profession, that the work study managers can refer to. Tradition, therefore, is transferred from one generation to the next.

All work study managers should consider seriously whether they are helping themselves or the company by issuing only standard times. Those who already go further than issuing standard times should review their system and confirm its value. Managers should ask to see the data that supports the standard times, to see if having access to it, or copies, could be useful to them.

Consistency of Standard Times

A vital aspect of any system of work measurement, and standard times, is *consistency*. There are a number of reasons why this is particularly important.

1   The ever changing structure of work.
2   The use to which the data is put.
3   The interest of people in the times, especially when it affects their pay.

It has long been accepted that in the measurement of work an absolute accuracy is not possible. It has also been long accepted, that, even allowing a band for error, establishing times and subsequently controlling them is a complex task. Proof of this is widespread, and can be seen in most companies, simply by studying operator performances.

> Performances of 80 are low and unlikely.
> Performances of 90 are really quite good.
> Performances of 100 should be the most common.
> Performances of 110 could be fairly frequent.
> Performances of 120 few and far between.
> Performances of 130 or above – something wrong!

It is quite possible for a company with performances averaging 100 to have high wages and good industrial relations, and for a company with average performances of 130 to have lower wages, and poor industrial relations. Indeed, in the longer term, the first company will be more able to continue a high wage system.

The major point being emphasised here is that a system based on *consistent* times will inevitably produce a sound pattern of performances. As soon as *inconsistencies* are allowed to spread, then performance patterns will begin to change. Performances will begin to move upwards in a haphazard manner. Industrial relations will begin to suffer.

Whenever there is a dispute concerning times, usually related to bonus pay, it is almost inevitable that *inconsistency of times* will emerge as a major, if not the only, cause.

Any management that leaves the establishment and maintenance of times entirely to management services has delegated a terrible responsibility to another department. Lack of co-ordination, lack of understanding from management and lack of authority for management services means that the responsibility placed on them is an almost impossible goal. This results in ever more inconsistencies and increasing problems. The management services department that has achieved success without the total commitment and support of management is rare indeed. This book does not recommend that the management service department is given authority, *but that management who already have authority should not opt out of their responsibility of ensuring that standard times are consistent.* It is regrettable, perhaps, but simply employing a professional management services manager will not guarantee consistency of times. Management policy, understanding, co-operation and responsibility are essential ingredients.

The Trade Union View

As a general rule, the trade unions will support work study applied well, and react to it when badly applied. There is, from the trade union movement, respect for integrity, and respect for management, when consideration is given to its members. If one accepts that management becomes responsible for standard times, *through* management services, safeguards of impartiality remain. The Code of Ethics and Professional Practice of the management services profession still demands the thoughtful consideration and impartiality that leads to a high degree of consistency. To this extent a management services professional cannot become a 'company man'.

There have been many occasions when to the surprise of management existing staffing levels were found to be *too low* following a measurement exercise. In such cases, there is no choice for the work study department but to recommend increases in staffing and cost. Professional standards demand that those qualified facts are identified.

On the other hand, employees and trade unionists often hold back on effort and co-operation when being studied. This is an instinctive and protectionist act, rather than one of dishonesty. If we are honest with ourselves, we all react out of character, when being closely observed by someone who is almost a stranger.

There are many ways to optimise earnings opportunity, besides attempting to manipulate standard times. However, if the times themselves are *inconsistent*, it is natural that employees and their union representatives will try to bring them back into balance. Management should not be surprised, or even consider it wrong, if unions or employees try to correct inconsistencies that should not be there in the first place.

A 'New' Basis for Trust

The views of both management and the trade unions should take second place to consistent standards. *A different way should be found to share benefits*. The professional should be used as a basis of integrity and trust between management and unions.

The first priority, when introducing work study, must be to create a sound working relationship between the department, its employees and the visitors. The objectives shown in fig. 9 may prove a useful guide.

DEPARTMENT				VISITORS	
Management		Operators		Management Services	
Managers Foreman	Supervisors Assistants	Operators	Union Reps	Work Study Managers & Section Leaders	Work Study Practitioners & Trainees assisting management
To plan production To meet targets To control production cost quality safety Std. Times To solve problems To train To improve productivity To maintain good industrial relations	To assist in the running of the Department	To produce output/ service in relation to defined targets methods quality safety	To act as a liaison with operators/ management in whichever area it arises (within a terms of reference)	To advise To control own staff To train own staff To maintain professional standards To design incentives with management	To improve productivity (methods/ layout) To supply control data (for accounts, planning, training) To implement incentives To maintain incentives To assist or advise management or operators

Fig. 9   The overlapping objectives of contributing employees.

Further Guidelines for Meetings Involving Work Measurement

Using the application of incentives as an example, fig. 10 is suggested as a possible format for a pattern of discussions. In the main, Stages 1, 2 and 3 are preliminary, though formal. Stages 4, 5 and 6 are a continuing series of informal discourses. Stage 7 returns to formality, and is concerned with the termination of introducing the standard times.

It is advisable to spend a little too much on communications, rather than not enough. You can always cut back on this expenditure, if it proves to have been excessive. No psychological damage will have been done. If management starts

35

	Present	Basis of Discussion

Stage 1	Manager & Foreman
	Work Study Manager or
	Section Leader
	Work Study Practitioner(s)
		Purpose of Exercise.
		Quality of Measurement.
		Terms of Reference.
		Targets (Completion).
		Methods to be used.
		The need to take x studies.
		The need for qualified operators.
		Implications of exercise –
		          Advantages
		          Disadvantages
		The need for subsequent
		          maintenance.
		Security arrangements for employees.
		Any other problems or points.

	Present	Basis of Discussion
Stage 2	Manager & Foreman Work Study Practitioner(s) Union Representative(s)	As above in the preliminary steps, but with a slightly different approach. Here one has agreed provisionally the aims within Company policy, and the means. The discussion is to explain and to create an atmosphere of co-operation. Information, and the implications of the exercise are, therefore, of particular interest and importance.
	Present	Basis of Discussion

Stage 3	Manager & Foreman
	Work Study Practitioner(s)
	Union Representative(s)
	Supervisors and Operators
		Almost a repeat of Stage 2
		but incorporating any changes
		made, or clarifying specific
		points on: Purpose
		                 Implications
		                 Targets
		Gain agreement to commence or
		continue discussion.
		Revised paperwork systems, if any.

	Present	Basis of Discussion
Stage 4	Work Study Practitioner(s) Supervisors Operators	Discuss any points raised by supervisors or operators, such as timing, rating, reasons for x studies. Thank supervisors and operators for assistance. Ensure a good flow of necessary information takes place, e.g. about work to be studied.

Fig. 10   Suggested patterns of discussion when introducing time study and
incentives.

	Present	Basis of Discussion
Stage 5	Work Study Practitioner(s) Union Representative(s)	Discuss any matters of interest or concern, as they arise. Involve Manager, Supervisors or Operators if helpful.
	Present	Basis of Discussion
Stage 6	Work Study Practitioner(s) Manager/Foreman Union Representative(s)	Explain any delays with reasons and revised targets. Discuss Job Breakdowns and their revision where necessary. Issue and discuss Set-Up Sheets. Discuss any desirable change in Method. Any Problems. Issue Standard Times supported by Job Breakdown and Set-Up Sheets.
	Present	Basis of Discussion
Stage 7	Manager & Foreman Work Study Practitioner(s) Union Representative(s) Supervisors Operators	Discuss the Standard Times. Discuss implications of using times. Security arrangements, possibly retraining. Any problems. Outline any opportunities. Explain rights to Check Studies. Explain how system functions.

Fig. 10 cont.

by economising on communications, and subsequently decides to increase, much damage has already been irretrievably done.

Consistency and Time Study

In the early part of this century, P.M.T.S. was developed as a means of replacing the inconsistencies of time study. Indeed, consistency was one of the *stated* prime objectives at the development of P.M.T.S. This does not prove that time study need be inconsistent; it merely recognised that it usually was, and in fact still is today. On the other hand, when the basis of the job is inconsistent, then even P.M.T.S. cannot produce a consistent time. Such facts should be known to all.

Chapter Three

The Concept of Work Standards

In all spheres of human activity, we measure the world around us. We are able to measure distance, length, areas and volumes, and we have precisely defined units of measurement capable of precise comparison.

A litre	A metre
A foot	A hectare
A pint	A pound

No carpenter would consider making a table without his measuring instruments (his rule and square, for example).

What greengrocer would dare to sell many of his goods without having a scale to hand? Indeed, even if he would, who amongst us would buy unweighed goods such as potatoes or tomatoes from him?

Of even greater importance is the measurement of time. Time is a measure of our very life span, and everything we do.

A man gets up at 7.00 a.m. so that he will have sufficient time to wash, dress, and have breakfast before catching the 7.45 a.m. bus to work. He works five days in every week from 8.15 a.m. until 4.30 p.m. with one hour for lunch. He sometimes misses the 4.45 p.m. bus, and as a result must wait twenty minutes for the next one. He knows this, and checks it with his own watch. Four weeks in every year he receives a holiday with pay. Even his pay will have been affected by the number of hours worked.

At home, his leisure time is governed by time. The football match on Saturday starts prompt at 3.00 p.m., and, since it will take half an hour to get to the ground and into a good position, he leaves home at 2.30 p.m.

In fact, this orderly control of life by time can make life much easier. In many respects, life would be chaos without it.

We can see then that nearly every activity of our life, from the cradle to the grave, is controlled or at least affected by time.

The Structure of Work

In society there are a number of naturally occurring structures. Each of these structures can be broken down to different levels, or even built up from basic components.

Consider language first, and this can be any language.

The alphabet   A small number of letters or symbols, perhaps 20–30.

Words   There is a limited number of these each with a limited meaning (i.e. what is contained in the dictionary).

Sentences   Infinite in number, and each one limited in meaning.

Paragraphs   Again unlimited, but with an opening up of meaning.

Books   Unlimited in number but with an area of knowledge.

Libraries   Back to a small number, but very complex and containing a sea of knowledge.

Other naturally occurring structures in society have a similar basis to language. A brief conceptual comparison is shown in fig. 11.

LANGUAGE	MATERIAL WEALTH	THE ECONOMY (WORK)
Alphabet	Elements	Basic Human Motions
Words	Materials (Raw)	Elements (Time)
Sentences	Combined Materials	Standard Times
Paragraphs	Products	Standard Costs
Books	A system (A home)	Profit & Loss Accounts
Libraries	Life itself	The Economy

Fig. 11   Conceptual comparison of naturally occurring social structures.

Language

Language is dependent upon alphabet, words and sentences to be meaningful. One can study the beauty and art of language in the form of *literature*, but surely not without a sound basis in *grammar* theory. How could the author, or communicator, survive, if someone kept changing the meaning of words, *but did not keep the dictionary up to date?*

Material wealth

Material wealth is dependent at three levels on the elements, raw materials, and the combination of materials into products. Although there is a limit to the number of basic elements, one can make endless combinations of them to produce new materials. The chemist must understand the elements and chemical structure analysis in order to produce new materials. The scope for the designer is considerably widened *because of the work of the chemist.* Yet, so often, it is the work of the designer alone that receives the acclaim.

The economy

Basic human motions, elements and standard times are at the basis of the economy. Naturally, machines are important, but there is a long way to go before machines and computer take over. Even if the computer and machine do take over large sections of the economy, people will still have work to do. *It is not possible fully to understand work, unless one understands the basis of human movement.* Work measurement is the most effective means by which this understanding can develop. The stability of the economy is largely dependent on a solid labour foundation.

The management services officer deals with basic human motions, elements, and standard times. *This is equivalent to grammar in language.*

The manager and accountant deal with standard times, budgets, plans and profit and loss accounts. Directors, politicians and civil servants deal with profit and loss accounts, strikes, unemployment and the economy. *This is equivalent to literature in language.*

It is all too easy for people working at one level to overlook the significance of another level. This applies in both directions.

Measurement at Work

The management of industry, commerce, hospitals and education is just as subject to the demands of time as any aspect of life. To establish a system of order and control, information about how long work takes is used. This is either estimated, analysed from past records, or measured. The art of measuring work is known logically as *work measurement*.

Unlike the measurement of weight, length, volume and minutes, which to some extent are international standards, we are concerned with how long it takes to complete a task, any task. There are hundreds of thousands of tasks; indeed new tasks are being thought up and introduced every day. Change is continuous and inevitable.

The concept of work measurement is not really new, though it has only crystallised in recent years. The acceptance of 'control' in our lives is not new. Sports, meals, meeting at the pub and closing time are all forms of control. Control is needed and used in places of employment too. It is irrelevant who runs an organisation; even with worker control detailed planning and control is necessary. Any form of pre-planning will require a knowledge of how long different tasks are likely to take.

In the modern complex society, work measured by specialists has frequently replaced subjective thinking or past records by introducing a whole new range of techniques. These can cover most different types of work situation.

The use of a time scale to co-ordinate the efforts of large groups of human beings, plus machines, materials and services, is unavoidable. It is vital that the times are both acceptable and consistent.

Measurement of a Task

Just how long might it take to complete a task, say 'assemble a motor'? Clearly it will depend upon a number of factors:

1 the design of the motor;
2 the method of assembly;

41

3   any mechanical and/or power aids;
4   the effort and skill of the operator.

There may be several other factors as well.

Before we can determine how long this job takes, we must define exactly what we mean. Below are listed some useful definitions.

B.S. 3138 1979 WORK MEASUREMENT NO. 10004
The application of techniques designed to establish the time for a *qualified worker* to carry out a *task at a defined rate of working*.

The logical starting point is first to define the task that is to be measured. In the definition of time study the task or job is referred to as the *specified elements*.

The job may be specified in a number of ways. The training officer may prepare a task analysis. The work study officer will prepare a work specification or an element description (job breakdown). The job would be considered to be a cycle of work.

B.S 3138 1979 WORK SPECIFICATION NO. 51003
A document setting out the details of an operation or job, how it is to be performed, the layout and the workplace, particulars of machines, tools and appliances to be used, and the duties and responsibilities of the worker.

N.B. The standard time or allowed time assigned to the task should be included.

B.S 3138 1979 WORK CYCLE NO. 42001
The sequence of elements which are required to perform a task or yield a unit of production. The sequence may sometimes include occasional elements.

In actual fact this is written out as a element description or job breakdown, but we will discuss this in detail in Chapter Six.

The next requirement is to find an operator who is qualified to perform the job as it is described. One does not *necessarily* merely describe what the operator does.

B.S. 3138 1979 QUALIFIED WORKER NO. 51001

One who is accepted as having the necessary physical attributes, who possesses the required intelligence and education and has acquired the necessary skill, and knowledge, to carry out the work in hand to satisfactory standards of safety, quantity and quality.

In reality this means that the operator has not only been selected and trained but has also had the opportunity to acquire a rhythmic and habitual method of performing the authorised job.

Compare this person to someone learning to drive a car. Having taken lessons for some time, the instructor decides that the trainee is ready to take the test. Assume for the sake of simplicity that the trainee passes the test first time. He would now be *trained* and *authorised* to drive alone, yet he will not have reached the peak of his ability to drive well. After a time with ample driving practice, the driver should gain in both confidence and competence. A time would come when he might be assessed as a good driver, perhaps to be judged by the advanced motorist's test.

Measuring the Time Alone is not Enough

The greater the understanding about the job, and thus recorded detail, the easier it is to assess whether an operator is qualified. Simply to measure the passing of time using a stopwatch is really not good enough. This will merely tell us how long the job took by that operator on that occasion. Even allowing for skilled rating assessment this will not guarantee the correct method or time.

When taking studies, in order to provide the management with such important data, the method observed should be the one approved by management. This point is extremely critical in time study. Often, the method observed is assumed, by manager and work study officer, to be acceptable. This is not necessarily the case, as there may be many hidden possible improvements. The operator may use one method as normal, a second method during work measurement, and a third method when on bonus!

The professional rule is that studies are not taken unless the operator is qualified, and one cannot judge the operator to be qualified or not unless the job is specified adequately.

Importance of Sound Data

This may seem like an over-emphasis, but at the extreme we are considering the causes of hundreds, perhaps thousands, of millions of pounds in lost production, bankruptcies, unemployment and lowered standards of living.

Once it is known how long jobs take, the cost of labour can be worked out without difficulty. From this, prices are calculated. Numbers of employees at different grades can be established, and machines utilised to an optimum. Effective space utilisation soon becomes possible. Production is more closely planned and stock control enhanced. Few people would dispute that it is the main function of management to plan, to co-ordinate and to maintain some degree of order.

What happens in the situation where job times are not known? Alternatively, jobs which have predicted times may take more or less time than expected. Life is much easier in the organisation where everyone *agrees* on how long a job should take and it is indeed completed in that time. As reaching agreement may be difficult, due to different priorities, it can be valuable to employ a professional specialist who is quite unbiased. Even then, not everyone will agree, certainly initially, but at least the basis of the discussion is carefully prepared.

Rating

Another point of contention during the study is the human variation in skill, effort, dexterity, concentration etc. To overcome this particular cause of time variation, a means of assessment known as rating is used.

This means that an adjustment is made to the observed time to allow for human variation. Someone who is working clearly very effectively would be given a good assessment, and someone not really trying would be given a poor assessment. Chapter Five has been devoted to this subject. Suffice it to say for the moment that rating is necessary during time study to allow for this inherent variation.

There are nationally accepted standard rating films. These have been shown to people from all parts of the world, with little training. It is quite remarkable that, whatever their nationality or background, there is a high degree of consistency. This confirms the theory that rating is essentially applied from a human instinctive point of view.

Relaxation at Work

A further and very significant feature of the concept of work standards is that of rest. It is internationally accepted that the human being is not capable of a sustained effort for hours on end. On the other hand, employment is best organised by asking people to attend places of employment during agreed periods, e.g. eight hours/day, five days/week.

Frederick Taylor, at the turn of the century, demonstrated the value of organised rest periods. The need to rest has gained worldwide recognition, and is supported by modern medical research.

After carefully measuring how long the operator should take, whilst working, one must recognise the need to rest by allowing a percentage on top of the work time. It is thus recognised that a unit of work consists of both work and rest.

In one very interesting project, the management of a weaving shed were concerned to increase output. An activity sample showed that for a considerable proportion of the day the looms were lying idle. Thirty operators were employed on 300 looms, and the operators needed rest. Hence in agreement with management they simply stopped the looms for relaxation for 16 per cent of the day. A solution in this case was to provide five more operators. In this way thirty operators kept the looms working throughout the day whilst five operators in turn took rest pauses. Direct labour cost per unit remained as before, but the use of capital was much improved.

To cover adequately all complex work situations, there is a series of allowances. Each is different, in nature and purpose. All nevertheless have the same objective: to ensure that everything the operators are asked to do has been allowed for, in the time allocated to the job. No stone should remain unturned, and the times should be equally acceptable to both management and unions.

The Standard Unit of Work

The aim of work measurement, in most instances, is to produce a unit of time related to a specific job. This time is to be issued to various departments within the organisation. This is known as the *standard time*.

Each standard time is made up of standard units of work. In the same way that a coffee table may be 14 *inches* high, assembling a coffee table may take 27.5 *standard minutes* to complete.

B.S. 3138 1979 STANDARD UNIT OF WORK NO. 43031
A unit of work consisting of basic time plus relaxation allowance and contingency allowance where applicable. In current practice, 60 or 1 standard units are produced in one hour when unrestricted work is carried out at standard performance.
N.B. Standard unit of work is expressed in terms of standard minute or standard hour.

It has never been fully clear in Britain who is responsible for work standards. No one doubts that management is responsible for *methods*, but responsibility for *times* varies from company to company. Perhaps in the majority of cases management services are responsible for standard times.

This is a controversial topic, and quite possibly the wrong decision has been made. It is this particular decision, this particular responsibility, that is costing Britain hundreds of millions of pounds a year. Standard times are prepared by work study to cover a specified method. That method is 'controlled' by management, and the times issued by management.

The Co-ordinating Role of Management

Management are not subservient to the engineers. Engineers report to management, though they are governed by engineering principles. Management are not subservient to the accountants. Accountants report to management, though they are governed by professional practice. The same applies in the case of computers, personnel, and even, with reservations, trade unionists. *Management must be responsible*.

Hence, though the preparation of standard times may be delegated as a *professional responsibility* to management services, the management should be responsible for the quality and maintenance of those times.

It could be suggested, and with good cause, that management have not recognised this responsibility for too long. The result is that the very foundation stones of many companies are extremely unstable.

A Brief National Survey

In Britain today, standard times are very widely used as the basis of incentive schemes. Here are millions of times being used for jobs that are significantly inaccurate. As the jobs have been changed, the times have been untouched. It would probably be very surprising to discover how many jobs have been changed by management, or have been known to them to have changed, but the original times retained. In some circumstances this is not vital. *If for example the operators, not on bonus, produce more output for the same wage, then the manager is to be congratulated*. When output is linked to bonus, however, and the time is not changed, extra output results in an increased wage, stagnant direct costs, and a lower overhead cost per unit. Again, the first reaction to this is one of congratulation. Yet it has resulted in cementing in direct cost, even though improvement was made at the direct place of work. The manager in this case has also introduced, or accepted, wages anomalies, and a psychological position where the employee wishes to protect his earnings. When later someone tries to improve methods, the employees will bitterly resent any change, as a formal method improvement is normally followed by work measurement, reducing the standard times. Unless this is done, *management cannot gain the full benefit of the method change*. If this is done the operators may have their bonus earning opportunity cut. As stated in the chapter on industrial relations, operators will resist change when all they see is benefits to the company, and disadvantage to themselves. *Who can blame them?*

Clearly this cannot be a satisfactory situation, and an alternative approach should be sought. This is really quite simple to achieve, but is considered to be outside the scope of this book. Suffice it to say that only two major aspects are considered to be vital in this instance:

1 management philosophy on work measurement;
2 the structure of the bonus payment scheme.

Many companies change from a non-bonus situation to a bonus situation without being aware of the long-term implications. The initial application of incentives will probably be very successful, compared to past performance. After two or three years, however, the problems *will emerge*. By then it is already too late. It does sound rather unpleasant, but it is like cancer – by the time it is discovered, it is usually too late.

Naturally, the managers will eventually conclude that it is the fault of the incentive scheme. After all, the problems did not exist in quite the same way before. On the other hand they will not wish to withdraw the incentive scheme! *Prevention is better than cure!*

A Set of Simple Rules

How wise is the company that understands both the benefits and the problems of work measurement and incentive schemes. In understanding the problems, they are able to take the classic preventative measures with confidence:

1 method study;
2 sound work specifications;
3 qualified operators;
4 highly experienced work study staff;
5 maintenance of methods *and times* as the responsibility of management;
6 a ceiling on bonus earnings.

There are said to be some reasons why this list should be modified! These will be put forward by some executives when introducing work study. A favourite is to put in incentives first, based on the present methods, thus gaining the early benefits of increased output. Method study can be completed later. *This is a short-term temptation that is best resisted.*

Temptation to use a Short-term Approach

In the first place, methods are likely to be highly variable. There may be no present method, just lots of present methods. The major benefit of accepting work study, to the employees, is the higher earnings from bonus. This will be quickly earned, as expected, and indeed exceeded, by introducing their own new methods. They will, however, expect to keep the 'old' times. With what does management then pay for co-operation in method study?

The first economic argument of quick returns has some validity. Incentive schemes can be very lucrative, and will probably also be demanded quickly by the unions. After all they can see the rewards from higher earnings. For a year or two, perhaps, management and unions, having the same objective, can work 'in accord'. Once nicely settled, *higher earnings become the reason for withdrawing co-operation, and the basis for demanding more.* Rate cutting will be strongly opposed by the unions, quite rightly too. In addition to this, management may feel that as methods are soon to be changed as a matter of policy, why spend too much time preparing sound work specifications? Yet this is the only basis they have for changing standards. The cry then is for speed of application. *This pressure should be resisted.*

A Basic Premise

Few people understand how to prepare a really thorough work specification, and it is very time-consuming. The better the specification, the greater the experience required to prepare it, and hence the higher the salaries to be paid. Add to this the fact that things keep on changing, and updating can seem a problem. Yet it is those same changes that are the major reason for keeping precise detail. When change occurs, it can be shown to have occurred. Standard times are usually protected for the employees by the following: *No standard time will be changed unless methods, equipment, materials, conditions, or anything else, changes or unless there is shown to be an error of calculation.*

It is essential that some means of quantifying the change has been kept on record.

Before incentives this was not quite so important. In many companies, bonus earnings are 'out of hand' because change has taken place, but cannot be shown to have taken place. Hence, in accordance with the standard agreement shown above, there is no basis for changing the standard times. Management would be wrong to try. This is how wages drift has occurred, as a result of incentives. *Quality of work measurement must be a priority; control and maintenance essential.*

If the work specification was not properly prepared, how is the work study officer to decide if the operator is qualified or not? In any case unions, managers and accountants all want this vital data 'now', hence the work study officer feels obliged to take but a few quick studies, and issue the times. Within weeks of working on incentives, for the first time, or on a new method, the operator will be 'more qualified' than ever before. Already the standard times are out of date. *The manager must be responsible.*

Initial Assessment of Times

Traditionally, standard times are first issued to the manager and through him to the operators. It is well known that both will think the times rather unfair as targets for output. This view is inevitably expressed by the operators and very frequently by the manager, though in private. Within weeks or months everyone will *know* that the targets can be achieved, as the operators will work consistently at or above 100 performance. The management will make no comment about their earlier reservations. At the next issue of standard times, however, they will probably once again suggest that the times are too tight. No criticism is intended here, but emphasis is made because this view is so very widespread, even if mistaken.

In earlier years, targets were issued at a 75 performance, and it was easy to see how these times could be 'beaten': i.e. 1.33 normalised minutes (at 75 performance) equals 1.00 standard minute (at 100 performance).

Thus times issued at 75 performance *appear* more acceptable than times issued at 100 performance. Many managers appreciate the full significance of the 'defined level of performance', but surprisingly, even today, many do not.

Standard performance should be the average not the minimum.

Virtually all experienced work study managers are aware of this, and the reasons why, but they need to conform to company policy, and must respond to the demands of management. They will also know, in the main, how to avoid the problems, but are not consulted. Policy has already been determined. The managers then often press for things to be completed 'in the normal hurry', blissfully unaware of the problems they are precipitating. Having had no faith in work study from the outset, it is all too obvious where the fault lies when things go wrong. *Greater understanding is a vital ingredient.*

Apathy of Work Study Officers

Given this background, which is the norm rather than the exception, work study officers themselves begin to take an apathetic view. There is known to be an attitude amongst some officers that you move to the next company and promotion before the storm breaks. Newcomers to the profession often do not join because of the status and respect offered, but drift in by accident. Some are even promoted to a position of responsibility that is above their ability. The talent, and motivation, to promote the true value of the profession is thus weakened.

The percentage of really experienced and dedicated work study officers in this country is thus critically low. *Therefore, the right level of practitioner should be demanded.*

Blind Acceptance of Standard Times

There is probably not an accountant in the country who will question the data provided by work study. Indeed it would be wrong to question quality, when the responsibility is invested in another department. Hence, no matter how wrong the data is, it is the responsibility of the accountant to ask for and to use it.

Fig. 12 is intended to be thought-provoking, and readers are encouraged to question the validity of the principles shown.

WORK STUDY (MANAGEMENT SERVICES)	MANAGEMENT ACCOUNTS	FINANCE
Skilled evaluation needed. Hundreds of solutions to choose from. Considerable 'human' implications THE TRUE BASIS OF COST LIES HERE { Speed of Output (SMs) Plant Utilisation Power consumed/unit Space needed/unit Support staff needed Materials needed (Value Analysis) Materials utilisation } Status, training and ability of Work Study Officer rarely matches the true responsibility of this Department. Reasons: Traditional, psychological, lack of knowledge, 'fear'	Essentially ANALYTICAL, and developed using 'unsophisticated maths' in the main. Very dependent for numbers on Management Services Accepting data from Management Services provides a basis of CONTROL only STANDARD COST { Labour (unit) Materials (unit) Overhead (allocated per unit) } BUDGET { Labour (totals) Materials (total) Overheads (total) Forecasts (total) } CONTROL exercised by comparing Actuals to Forecasts The role of Cost and Management Accounts should never be underestimated. It is a powerful, positive tool of management. It is not, however, so vastly complex that the average manager need be confused by its 'mystery'. Learn all about it and use it to your advantage.	1 Basic Human Motions ($\frac{1}{1000}$ s of a minute) 2 Elements ($\frac{1}{10}$ s of a minute) 3 Standard Times (minutes) 4 Standard Costs and Prices (hours) 5 Profit and Loss Accounts (staff) 6 The Economy When the pattern of motion is poor, all else that is built on that pattern must be poor. The accountant 'takes over' at the Standard Time. By then it is too late!

Fig. 12   The true basis of control.

The over-riding feature of Management Accounts is the quality of the basic data from which standard costs and budgets are developed. Never forget how wrong Management Services can be if they are not good at their job. How good can they indeed be, if it is a low salary, low status job? How good can they be if they have to do everything in a hurry, with little or no support from Management & Supervision?

Chapter Four

The Nature of Work

The first and perhaps most important characteristic of work is the wide variety of methods that may be employed in order to complete a job. Work as we can observe it today in the factory, office, hospital, indeed anywhere, is quite simply the *present method*.

It is unlikely that the method seen today has been in use unchanged for more than two years. It is equally unlikely that any method seen today will be in use unchanged two years from now. It is also unlikely that another company wishing to perform the same *function* will have selected the same method.

In historical terms work is constantly changing, though this is not so obvious day to day. Consider the implications for any organisation that begins to plan and control itself, using job times as a key feature, yet does not make total provision for the updating of those times as the job changes.

In Chapter Three a comparison was made between language structure and work structure. The importance of that concept is critical here in understanding the nature of work. In the same way that sentences and books are *infinite* in number, and constantly being renewed, so too are products, methods, and profit and loss accounts. In the same way that letters and words are of a *finite* nature, so too are certain aspects of work. Mainly this is true of basic human motions, but it is also largely true of elements.

The Basis of Work Characteristics

The first division of work could be said to be work done only by hand, or work done by machine. Work done by machine tends to have manual work also as part of the cycle. Some manual

sing tools or power tools, but this is easily
ory, the greater the machine time as a propor-
eater the control over the times. The object is to
e a work cycle into manual elements, and machine
ments.

The second division of work is the separation of those
elements that may be judged as repetitive and those that
occur occasionally. Whereas some repetitive types of job
are clearly going to repeat over and over again, such as
work on a conveyor belt, less obvious jobs have components of
repetition.

Consider first operators who are seated, or stand in the same
spot. They are working in the main with their hands, and there
is scope for building up repetitive motion. On the other hand,
people that need to walk about in order that their work can be
done lose the precision that their hands can develop. Their
work may be repetitive, such as operating a specific machine, or
non-repetitive. A feature of most non-repetitive work is that,
hidden well away, repetition can often be found.

For example, building a house is a non-repetitive job.

1 Laying bricks can be very repetitive.
2 Hammering nails, say in floor boards, can be very repetitive.

The actual house itself may be the only one of that design in
the whole world. Therefore, as a job, including many skills and
many complications, it may never be repeated again at any
time in the future. Even if the same house were to be built
on another site by the same builder, it is almost inevitable
that many things would be done differently. The job in total,
therefore, is called non-repetitive, but elements of the job are
called repetitive when they occur with a regular and high
frequency.

The third major division of work elements is the separation of
constant elements from variable elements. The constant element is one where the time taken to perform that task will *tend to
remain a constant*, given certain constraints. The variable element
is one where the time is expected to vary in relation to some
characteristic(s). For example you might expect the time to

54

walk one mile to remain fairly constant, just as running times remain fairly constant. If you ask the operator to carry different weights, however, it is clear that the time will increase as the weight increases. The ground surface, too, could well have an effect. A farm labourer would take more time to walk across a ploughed field than he would to walk the same distance by road.

It is probably the very changing nature of work, more than anything else, which makes work measurement so very difficult to do really well. It may also be the reason why it can become the basis for such a fascinating career.

By breaking cycles of work into smaller components of work, we can begin to understand much more deeply the nature of work itself. We call these smaller components of work *elements*. Hence, when preparing a description of the work, we take a work cycle, as we wish to study it, and divide it into its natural elements. The end result is normally called an *element description*. It is recognised that there are eight element types, but we shall consider just six to begin with. These are shown as three pairs, because they are essentially opposites.

> Manual   or Machine
> Repetitive or Occasional
> Constant   or Variable

It is possible to have one element type within a pair to influence its opposite. One example would be an operator cutting a piece of wood on a band saw. He is limited by the capability of the machine to some degree, and yet at the same time he controls the rate at which the cut is made. With experience the operator will 'feel' the optimum pressure needed to cut the wood. Hence the element is neither fully manual nor machine-controlled. For simplicity at this stage it is perhaps best to accept that each type is quite distinct and logical in its identification.

It is inevitable, however, for elements *outside* the pairs to be of more than one type. An element might thus be:

> 1 Manual/Occasional/Constant
> or 2 Manual/Repetitive/Variable
> or 3 Machine/Occasional/Variable

Of the remaining element types, oddly enough, the last two are not a pair of opposites.

The first is the *governing element*. In this case we have two elements occurring concurrently, the one, being longer than the other, governs the work cycle time at that point. The shorter of the two elements, incidentally, is known as *inside work*, but this is not an accepted element type. It is an anomaly!

The eighth and final element is not strictly speaking an element at all. It is known as a *foreign element*, and is really work observed during a study that is not approved by management. Assume a study is being taken, having already discussed the element description with management and had it approved. Part way through the study, the operator completes another element; this is recorded as an element, and the study continued. Later it may be judged that the manager should be consulted. Should this 'extra' element be allowed for or not? The manager may confirm that it should be done, and that it had been overlooked at the discussion. In this case it is added into the description of the job at the appropriate spot. If the manager says it should not have occurred, it is extracted as a foreign element. In some cases, it is self-evident that something which happened during the study should not be included; it can thus be left out without discussing it with the manager. It is either described briefly, and extracted, or it is sometimes transferred into ineffective time. To give a frivolous example, the operator may have stopped momentarily to buy a raffle ticket. To ensure that a study error can be calculated, this time must be recorded, and it is recorded as an element, but no one need know what occurred. It is quite simply extracted as ineffective time and forgotten.

An Illustrated Example of Element Types

The idea then is to observe the cycle of work to be studied, and sub-divide into smaller *natural* components of work. A very simple example could be that of making a cup of tea as shown in fig. 13. The object here is to illustrate the principle only. A slightly different analysis could have been made, but this is not important.

Job: Make cup(s) of tea		
1	Fill kettle and put on to boil	(Manual, repetitive, variable). It is perhaps variable dependent upon the amount of water
2	Boil Water	(Machine, repetitive, variable, governing)
3	Place out cup, saucer and spoon, whilst kettle is boiling	(Manual, repetitive, constant – per cup)
4	Put milk and sugar into cup. Again whilst kettle is boiling	(Manual, repetitive, constant – per cup)
5	Warm pot, put tea into pot, fill pot and switch off kettle	(Manual, repetitive, constant)
6	Wait for tea to brew	(Machine or process, repetitive, constant)
7	Pour tea and aside pot	(Manual, repetitive, variable – dependent upon number of cups)
8	Stir tea and drink	(Manual, repetitive, constant)

Tea Maker

1	3	4		5		7	8

2		6
Kettle		Pot

Fig. 13   An over-simplified example of a work cycle showing different types of element.

The Logic of Element Selection

If we consider element 1 for a moment, it can be clearly seen that the work involved is concerned with the kettle and the tap. The second element is also concerned with the kettle, but not the tap, and here control is being taken over by the power source used. It is the instant that the power takes over, switch on power, that one type of element ends and another begins. In this case two elements commence simultaneously. The

57

machine element 'boil kettle' starts simultaneously with placing out the cups. As both elements 3 and 4 will finish before element 2, they are said to be governed by element 2. This is quite logical. Element 3 is concerned with the 'tools' of the job, and element 4 with the materials, hence they are separated. *Using these principles for Category A times will cause trained personnel to arrive, almost inevitably, at the same element structure.*

To identify the precise end of each element, part of the cycle is separately selected as the instant at which one element ends and the next begins. This is called the *breakpoint*. Breakpoint selection is so fundamental to good time study that it is dealt with at great length later.

The Element as a Building Brick

In the same way that bricks are used to build useful structures, elements are also added together. The result of combining selected elements with allowances is the standard time. It is in this form that they are so very useful. Unlike the brick, however, the elements are different to each other and subject to frequent change. Elements, and thus standard times, could be said to be the basis of the economy. See fig. 14.

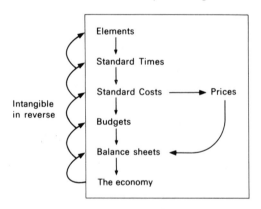

N.B. One can in fact go back one step to Basic Human Motions but these are always added into elements

Fig. 14   The link between elements of work and the economy.

It is quite true to submit that the skill with which these small items of work are prepared will ultimately affect the state of the company's balance sheet, and indeed the national economy. Of course, influence at economic level may ultimately affect the elements, but this would be an intangible analysis.

One of the largest mistakes made by companies is the belief that everything starts with the standard time, and that this is easily and cheaply prepared. *It does not, cannot, and never will!*

Human Engineering

To understand work, one has to understand human engineering, production engineering, and the working of the mind. To send someone out with a stopwatch and a fortnight's training is almost irresponsible. Five years' training would not only be more appropriate, but in the long term prove to be the most economic. In other words, trainees *with only 2–3 years' experience* should be closely supervised.

Selecting the Measurement Technique

Before one considers more deeply whether time study is the most appropriate method for measuring work, one must look at the over-all picture.

There are a number of entirely different situations in which one might wish to have work measured. It should always be remembered that time study is only one technique available, amongst a whole group. The different techniques overlap one another.

For highly repetitive manual work, one can use time study quite easily, but first or second level pre-determined motion time systems are probably more appropriate.

Synthetic data has a wide range of uses but requires time study or *P.M.T.S.* to provide the base data in the first instance. This is widely used in engineering, but even now it is not developed to its full potential.

For general work of a fairly repetitive nature, cycles from minutes up to hours, and where there are machine or process times to consider, time study is probably best.

59

As the nature of the work cycles becomes less repetitive, and involves several operators or machines, then systematic sampling will begin to play a role.

For work of a non-repetitive nature one might consider activity sampling (random) or comparative estimating.

Even with the nature of work giving a useful guide, one also has to consider most carefully the purpose to which the data will be put when it is finally ready.

The Skill of the Practitioner

Each of the techniques has much to offer, and any company using work study would be wise to have people trained in *all* of them.

Assuming the staff are able to use all work measurement techniques, then their advice should be sought about the most appropriate technique to use in any given situation. It is essential, therefore, that the staff are qualified to advise.

This book has been devoted almost entirely to the practice of time study, and is intended to help in the understanding of this technique, *when it is the one chosen for any job*.

The Use of Time Study

Time study can be used in any of the following areas:

1   method study;
2   problem solving;
3   calculating standards;
4   providing synthetic data;
5   production studies (providing information);
6   check studies.

The two primary considerations about any work measurement technique to be used are:

1   the *purpose* for which the data is needed;
2   the *accuracy* required, and affected by *purpose*.

60

The Level of Accuracy

In method study, the amount of time allocated to problem solving is dependent upon the potential saving or benefit. The same rule applies in quality control and other fields. Fig. 15 illustrates the need to aim for an optimum level of service. Too little attention is just as bad as too much. The problem is deciding at which point to stop.

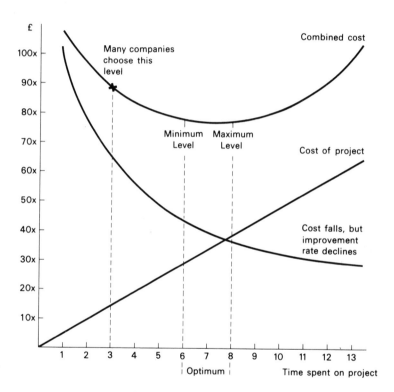

Fig. 15   A conceptual illustration of levels of study, showing that an optimum level exists.

The tendency in Britain is to save money on the *preparation* of standard times. There are cases when this is the right decision, but the number of loose standards and exceptionally high bonus earnings in this country is monumental. If this were a small problem, this book would never have been written. If only the facts could be made known – but they are not. Consider a butcher running his own business. Weighing meat to the nearest milligram is impractical, hence he may allow a minute fraction of meat surplus in one case, and short in another. The effect on both himself and the customer is really of no consequence. What would happen to the butcher, however, over a very extended period, if unknown to him his scales were inaccurate in favour of his customers? As one can imagine, the customers in most cases will never know or never tell, but the effect on his profits may be considerable. This example is a fairly accurate description of the effect on many of our leading companies, who do not understand the technique of time study.

Who Chooses the Level of Accuracy?

Who decides on the level of accuracy of standard times ought to be a clear-cut issue. It is not. The decision lies with the work study department, in theory, but in practice it is very strongly influenced by management. The tragedy of this position is that the wrong level of accuracy is usually achieved. As can be seen in fig. 15, already discussed, one can either try to be too accurate, or not aim high enough. Both result in excess cost. Pressures from management to keep work study cost down, and the natural wish to have the data as quickly as possible means that most standards are not accurate enough, rather than too accurate. This explains why bonus performances in most companies not using a ceiling tend to rise well above the theoretically reasonable 100.

When a manager asks for a standard time to be completed by the end of the week, the work study department will normally conform. Even though they know it is perhaps better to take three or four weeks, the manager is the manager. They may have long since accepted that management have logically decided that speed is beneficial. They may have long since accepted that management have decided that low accuracy standards are the most economic way of applying work study.

They are almost certainly wrong. Management made the early decision when work study was first introduced. At that time they did not really understand, indeed still do not really understand, the long-term effects of doing the job badly. The current management view is probably based on their slightly biased view of work study, a lack of understanding of the implications, *and the fact that they are not responsible for the standards*. Work study is the department responsible for preparing the standard times, and all the problems that are associated with work study.

For too long, work study departments have accepted that responsibility as one of the major reasons for their being. In the same way that management are accepted as being responsible for method, they should also be responsible for standard times. This is the only way to bring the profession back into total respect. Many will argue that method study is rarely done these days, that all management want are standard times of dubious accuracy. The original philosophy that accurate standard times are best established on sound methods of working needs to be re-established.

The following section suggests the basis upon which the responsibility for standard times could be successfully transferred to management. *This is a relatively new concept, and should be very carefully considered and discussed before adoption.* Its success is largely dependent upon management training and total support. The financial benefits are beyond belief.

Inevitability of Method Change

It should always be remembered that *method* is very much dependent upon the degree of repetition. Make something just once, and the method will be almost made up as one goes along. Make a hundred units of the same thing, and the method will gradually improve as experience grows. Make a thousand units, and a relatively fixed method will emerge *eventually*. Make one hundred thousand, and the method will be affected by all sorts of factors outside the normal departmental approach. Perhaps a new machine will be bought specially. Perhaps the work will be divided into smaller sections and possibly set up as a production line. It is quite unbelievable that in setting out to manufacture one hundred thousand units the method will be determined from the first one, and then insisted upon by management as being the authorised method. Of course methods will be reviewed and improved.

Logically, therefore, the time that the job will take will vary during those early days, as will the skill of the operators. *Time is inevitably linked to method*.

Adopting Three Levels of Accuracy

There is one way, then, in which a certain logic can be introduced into the preparation of standard times, and a decision taken on the level of accuracy.

Consider that it was possible to accept that there were say *three* levels of accuracy, not just one. Consider too that once these levels were defined more closely, as well as the means by which they could be attained, judged and monitored, management be made responsible for selecting the level. The effect could be quite remarkable. If a manager selected a low level of accuracy when it would have been better high, he will be at least partly responsible for the consequences. No longer will companies have to shrug their shoulders and accept poor standards, simply because they '*have to have them*' as work study prepare them. Any company that adopts such a policy will automatically ensure overnight that its managers are deeply concerned about the times in which the company has to place so much faith. Work study practitioners will overnight find their work standards under inspection, and thus be obliged to work more professionally. In the longer term this will benefit management, unions and the country. Three possible categories are shown in fig. 16.

Clearly the suggested categories can be varied to suit individual company circumstances. It is the philosophy that is important. Until now there seems no record of such a system available to the general public. It is likely that many companies will already operate on similar lines, though if so it is not commonly known.

As a general rule this policy would also benefit from a ceiling on bonus earnings. Many are the arguments for and against

CATEGORY A – Very high accuracy ± 5%
Very high potential cost (and thus saving)
The greater the earlier inefficiency, the greater the saving that can be shown
Very considerable expenditure is anticipated on production. The production run will be long, hence there will be time for the operators to acquire extra skills, **AND TIME FOR SEVERAL METHOD CHANGES.**

Work Study Responsibility

1 Method Study first – formal report to manager
2 Thorough training of operators
3 Thorough Job Breakdown and Work Specification. Element Description authorised by manager
4 Consider issuing a temporary value, plus a running in allowance based on a learning curve
5 When operators are qualified, then thoroughly measure the work and discuss preparation with manager. When ready issue all relevant documents (copies) and Standard Times (withdraw temporary)
6 Regular checks to be made of method

Manager's responsibility

1 Discuss methods and contribute
2 Ensure training is thorough
3 Read Element Descriptions and Work Specs carefully and initial as satisfactory
4 Discuss allowances or temporary times
5 Advise when operators are qualified on new method
6 Discuss build up of times with Work Study
7 Issue times
8 Monitor methods – do not allow unauthorised methods – Have times altered with any changes he would like to see introduced

CATEGORY B – Medium Level Accuracy ± 10%
Medium potential Cost
High expenditure anticipated on production, but with the likelihood of the job terminating within a foreseeable time.

Work Study Responsibility

1 Adjustments to method rather than full method study. Discuss possibilities with manager
2 Thorough training for operators
3 Fairly thorough Job Breakdown, Element Description, and Work Specification, again authorised by manager
4 Fairly thorough work measurement, discussing with manager. When ready issue times and documentation to manager
5 Periodic review of job life, and methods. If it appears to be lengthening perhaps undertake a method study and reissue times

Manager's responsibility

1 Satisfy self that the methods are fairly sound
2 Ensure that the descriptions are thorough and operators trained
3 Discuss times with Work Study and issue
4 Monitor methods – do not allow unauthorised methods – Have times altered with any changes he would like to see introduced

CATEGORY C – Low level accuracy ± 20%
Relatively low level of expenditure on this job. Known and limited life cycle

Work Study Responsibility

1 Fairly thorough Element Description dependent upon job life. Manager can authorise or not as he wishes
2 Brief Measurement of job, as necessary.
Issue a **TEMPORARY VALUE** with a life limited by the number of units or days

Manager's responsibility

1 Just to place this job in Category C may be enough. The rest could be left to his own supervision and the Work Study Department
2 It would be essential that the manager actually asked for a Category C time, not *any time*

Fig. 16   Three possible levels of accuracy for time study.

65

this, but it is something that is easier to take away than to impose. A ceiling as a concept is best dealt with as a separate subject in its own right.

Who Decides the Philosophy?

As management consists of several layers, ranging from Directors down to first line supervisors, it is logical to suggest the layer at which the levels of accuracy concept is considered. Really, the philosophy behind this concept must be considered by Directors and senior executives. The managers who have to work within the system will undoubtedly have mixed feelings on the matter. They are going to consider the day-to-day implications it will have for them, as well as for the company. Directors and senior executives will be more concerned about what it can do for the company, and the employees in general. The effect it may have on individual managers is of lower importance, as this can be allowed for by management development. In other words, it must be expressed as a clearly defined policy. No assumptions can be made that everything is all right or will be; the subject is too important to leave to chance. Reference to the three levels of accuracy, called Category A, Category B and Category C, is made throughout the book.

Professional Acceptance of Levels of Accuracy

As a separate consideration to management philosophy, the professional standards of practitioners is also quite fundamental to consistency. At the present time, and into the foreseeable future, these standards are monitored by the Institute of Management Services. Practitioners are encouraged to join this Institute by most employers, and its qualifications are widely accepted. There can be no conflict between management philosophy and professional standards, when management seek to raise the standards. The general position today in time study training is that students are taught in class at two levels:

1 practical time study to category C level (though not stated);
2 theoretical concepts of higher level time study, through different timing methods, synthetic data development and the data bank concept.

Difficulty of developing further skills when at work is caused because only one level of accuracy is *recognised*. That level is referred to as 'an aim to achieve ± 5%'. As this aim is sometimes impractical, and sometimes impossible, there is an atmosphere of confusion in many situations. It is quite common for students at college to refer to the impossibility of attaining standards taught in class. This is an instinctive feeling based on experience. It is quite a sound conclusion. As an increasing number of companies begin to adopt the principle of authorising levels, the Institute will in time recognise the change, and incorporate this into the academic training programmes. It would be almost impossible for the Institute to press this concept onto unwilling companies. The initiative, therefore, must be a management one.

Chapter Five

The Rating Concept

A major concept in the measurement of manual work is the rate at which a person works. It is well known that each one of us is capable of working at different speeds or degrees of effort. Walking, the common example, has even had a number of words developed to indicate changes in rate; 'dawdling', 'strolling' and 'hurrying' are examples. It is also recognised that, when hurrying, the walker is motivated to get from one point to another more quickly. Strolling is a natural speed for walking, too, yet there is no urgency in the pace.

Consider the housewife cooking dinner on Christmas Day. Relatives are arriving any minute, and there is more preparation to do than normal. There is a natural concern that everything is well done, and a desire to have things ready by a certain time. Quite possibly on Boxing Day the rate at which dinner is prepared is less hurried.

Motivation and Pace of Work

Provided that a human being has a specific reason, or reasons, for getting something completed quickly, they will speed up the pace at which they work. If there is no particular reason for hurrying, it is equally natural to slow down to a more leisurely pace. Such changes are predictable, natural, and international. Everything depends upon the degree of motivation.

Yet there are paces of work which are so slow as to be very cumbersome, and paces of work which are so fast as to be exhausting. There is quite a widespread belief that operators tend to work at a fairly steady pace while working. The number of minutes in a day actually worked is more critical a factor.

Rating Scales

To enable human beings at work to be measured with some confidence, a system of rating assessments has been devised. Using words like 'hurrying' and 'strolling' may be fine for assessing walking pace, but this does not have a universal application for any task. The rating system is based on numbers.

The rating scale, as it is called, recognises two major levels of working in the first instance:

1 a normal pace of working;
2 a motivated pace of working.

The second pace of working is $33\frac{1}{3}$% faster than the first. It has been in use for many years, and has gained wide acceptance.

Over the years there have been a number of rating scales devised and used, but in the main they have this one common feature. In fig. 17 one can see several rating scales that have been in recent use, each having the two paces of working. It is

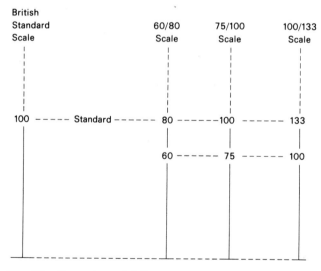

Fig. 17   Comparison of different rating and performance scales.

only in the British Standard Rating Scale that the normal pace is not shown, though it is accepted. Rating assessment is made to the nearest five.

Rating Concept and Incentives

It was inevitable that the rating scale concept and the structure of incentive schemes became linked. Nearly all modern incentive schemes based on output are linked to work measurement to provide the rate of working. To illustrate this point, the straight proportional scheme is shown in fig. 18 and careful note should be made of the horizontal axis. When an operator works at the motivated rate, he is judged to be working $33\frac{1}{3}$% faster than a normal rate, and will receive $33\frac{1}{3}$% extra money over base rate. Nevertheless, when working at the normal rate, he is considered to be working at a reasonable pace, or earning the base wage.

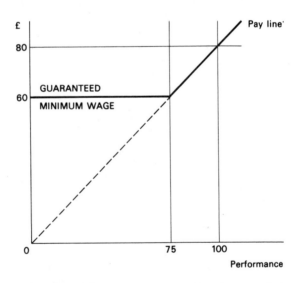

Fig. 18   The relationship between pay and performance in a straight proportional scheme.

Rating and Relaxation

In Chapter Three reference was made briefly to both rating and relaxation. No human being can work continuously at a high rate of working, or even the normal rate, without taking rest, and thus rest must be provided for the operator. When actually working, we assess an operator's rate of working using the rating concept. Once standard times have been issued, however, which include relaxation allowance, we judge the pace of the worker by calculating a performance. Hence, rating assessment is used as an instant assessment *in the preparation* of times, and performance is used to *judge the daily or weekly pace of working* after the times have been issued, and rest taken.

What is Rated?

So how exactly is this instant assessment of the rate of working of an operator while he is actually working made? This is a difficult question, with no precise answer. First let us consider *what* is to be judged, rather than how it is done. Speed of movement, effort, dexterity, and consistency are quoted as factors to be considered. Speed of movement, and effort, are surely partly related. How can an operator work with a fast speed of movement but a low effort? Of course, a person can stand still, but be holding a large weight. Here we have high effort, and no movement; yet how do you rate someone who is standing still? The next factor is dexterity, and how can that be judged? Finally there is the consistency of the operator. No doubt consistency, or even inconsistency, can be observed, but against which standard?

Complexity of Rating

Clearly, knowing the factors upon which one bases the judgement does not make rating easy. There is a British Standard definition for rating, so this should be examined.

B.S. 3138 1979 RATE, TO NO. 41027
To assess the worker's rate of working relative to the observer's concept of the rate corresponding to standard rating. The

observer may take into account, separately or in combination, one or more factors necessary to the carrying out of the task, such as: speed of movement, effort, dexterity, consistency.

Imagine the complexity of rating assessment, if an operator had a high speed of movement, was not too dexterous, and also worked inconsistently. Rating assessments are made at the rate of about five or six per minute. Furthermore, the work study officer has to make this assessment against his own concept of the rate, corresponding to standard rating, whatever that means!

Rating then, is not quite as simple as it first appears. Perhaps there is another idea which could offer a key to this problem.

Rating and the Qualified Worker

In our very first comments on time study, the definition was quoted. An extract from that definition is: 'to establish the time for a qualified worker to carry out specified elements'. Now if the elements are specified very thoroughly, and the operator is qualified at performing them, then he must have the appropriate dexterity, and will perform fairly consistently. Given a well-qualified operator, then all that has to be rated is speed of movement and/or effort. Dexterity and consistency can be assumed to be at a 100 rating equivalent.

Yet how does one judge when an operator is well qualified? There is only one way, in theory, and that is his ability to perform the specified elements. Here is another assumption. *The assumption is that the elements have been prepared with great skill on the part of the work study officer.* A direct comparison of the specified element can be seen actually being performed by the operator, with dexterity and consistency.

Basis of Sound Rating

If the manager is to authorise the element description as the basis of sound method, then all should be well.

1   The operator is using a method carefully considered by the manager.

2   The work study officer writes out a detailed element description, capable of judging the ability of the operator. Also, it is acceptable to the manager.
3   The work study officer takes a study, knowing from the description that the operator is well qualified. One must wait if necessary till qualified.
4   Rating assessment is based almost entirely on speed of movement or effort.

In this case, then, one can only be observing work that falls into categories A or B.

Acceptance of Poor Rating in some Circumstances

It is already known that category C work needs to be studied before the operator has the skills, and it is impractical to write out a detailed description, as the methods are sure to change. In other words, there are certain jobs of work performed by operators where rating assessment is almost impossible. It is fairly certain that in rating a category C job dexterity and consistency will be ignored. It is fairly certain that methods will improve, and so will skill. Hence when rating under these circumstances rating assessments will be generous. On the other hand it will take time for the operator to acquire these little extra skills, and the time issued has only a limited life anyway, so it does not matter too much. A tolerance of ±20% is allowed.

Misuse of Rating Skills

A risk taken by many companies is issuing *standard times* based on a category C preparation. It is almost totally certain that those times will quickly become loose. Because of the quality of preparation, particularly of the element description, these same times are not even maintainable. They very quickly offer bonus earning possibilities above that intended by the company, and become another area of inconsistency and discontent for someone else.

Companies can really only afford category C rating assessments when they are issuing category C or temporary times.

Emphasis of Sound Rating Opportunity

Consider next the accuracy of rating when preparing category A times. As just stated, the operator is working to a sound, authorised method. To facilitate long-term maintenance of the standard times, the element descriptions are thoroughly prepared. The manager is responsible for ensuring that method is adhered to, or if changed the standard times are changed.

When taking the studies, the work study officer first has to assess that the operator is qualified (in other words, can perform the specified elements with dexterity and consistency). Rating in such circumstances is infinitely more accurate than with an untrained operator. Speed of movement and effort rating is all that is needed.

Rating for Speed and Effort

The question arises once again: how does one rate for speed and effort? There is one answer, and one answer only. It is pure and natural instinct. Students from all over the world, following a short course, have shown an instinctive ability to rate for speed and effort. The research done in this area has been using nationally accepted rating films. The essential point to note here is the fact that in all these rating films the operators *are stated to be well qualified*. They never show the same operation being performed by different operators having different skills. It would be most interesting to see the results of rating exercises if the operators had different skills as well as different speeds.

Even so, the human being's instinctive ability at rating speed tends to be wrong. Some individuals rate extremely well, some are too generous, some too tight. Most people have a tendency to rate flat. This means tight rating over 100, and loose rating below the 100.

There are a number of natural trends that one can identify and these are illustrated in fig. 19.

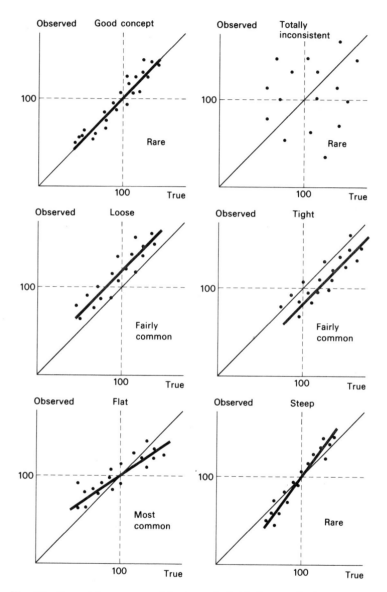

Fig. 19   Several known natural instincts. Individuals may display more than one tendency, e.g. tight and flat.

Training in Rating Skills

To train someone in rating skills, all one has to do is teach first the basic theory (rating concept, rating scales and factors involved). The trainee then watches a series of films and puts down his own concept of rating for each observation. These initial observations are then plotted against a 'correct' answer on a graph, and the trainee can see how far from true his instinctive assessment is. Next he must learn how to compensate for this error in future ratings. Clearly where there is a tendency to rate tight one loosens up. The adjusted ratings in subsequent film observations should show improvement on the graph. All this does in effect is to confirm to the person that his instinctive rating ability is still strong, and that he must continue to make the necessary adjustments. Special rating clinics are available to continue this throughout one's time study career. A guide to rating assessment is shown in fig. 20.

Rating (B.S.I.)	Guide to rating assessment
40 rating	Never seen! Too uncomfortable. It is harder to do this than work at 100.
60 rating	Rather slow and clumsy. Appears to make an effort to work slowly. Rarely seen except when taking studies.
80 rating	Nice steady pace. No noticeable hurry. Fairly natural pattern of movement, though occasional hesitation. Clearly knows the authorised method.
100 rating	Brisk pace. Operator seems fairly keen to complete the job quickly. Demonstrates skill and consistency in the authorised method.
120 rating	Hard pace of working. Needs practice and skill, even to be able to work at this speed. Usually, only seen on highly repetitive work.
140 rating	Intensely concentrated. Very high degree of skill. Can only be sustained for very short spells. Rarely seen.
160 rating	Seen perhaps once in a life time. Virtually impossible to attain. Perhaps possible with superskill. Certainly not possible on effort alone.

Always rate to the nearest 5.

Fig. 20 An imprecise table which may be useful when making rating assessments.

Finally, when actually taking a time study, one should rate according to the accuracy level chosen by the manager. For categories A and B, the operator should be judged to be qualified *before* any studies are taken. For category C, the operator can be rated at once, but only a temporary time is issued.

Chapter Six

Element Description

Element description is quite emphatically the most important part of time study. It is also the part that is generally completed with the least skill.

Effect of Poor Description

Failure to do description well will almost certainly cause the whole system to collapse. This may take one year, two years, even five years, but it will fail. There are two reasons for this inevitable failure:

1   the acceptance of the times;
2   the validity of the times.

For a Job with a Short Life

Assume in the first instance that a time was prepared in a logical and economic manner. In other words, where the work cycle involved has a brief and limited life, the time could be prepared quickly. The operator would be given the benefit of the doubt on any minor points, and improving methods would be ignored. The time issued *will quickly become obsolete*, as the job itself comes to an end. Hence during its life it will probably be acceptable to manager and employee, and will be valid in the circumstances.

For a Job with a Long Life

The more important times are those for jobs which have a significantly longer life span, and will consequently incur greater cost. To be truly valid, throughout the life of the job, the time must be amended as methods, equipment or conditions change. How can a time for a specified method remain valid, once the method has changed? How can it be said to be acceptable? It cannot be acceptable to the employee if the job time increases but the time issued stays. It cannot be acceptable to management if the job time increases or decreases; after all, the basis of pricing, cost control, training, indeed everything has been weakened. *To be acceptable to management, the time can only be based on the authorised method.*

Wages Drift and Incentives

Hence, if the management authorises, or even accepts (implied authorisation) a method change, without having the time corrected, it cannot be truly acceptable or valid. *Prior to incentives* it would have been reasonable. The extra output gained would have immediately resulted in a fall in unit cost. After all, when output is increased but wages remain the same cost per unit falls.

This is no longer true once incentives are introduced. When output rises following a method change, but the time is not changed, then a rise in wage for the operator will take away much of the benefit of the change. This is a small but vital fact which appears to have escaped the notice of many of our managers. *They are so accustomed to changing method without having to tell anyone that they continue to do so.* Any manager that does this, either deliberately or by implication, is responsible for allowing inconsistencies in earning power to develop. This will, without doubt, result in anomalies and quantifiable comparisons, which will lead to dissatisfaction. If such changes are allowed to consolidate, and work study not requested to update the time, at the time of the change, *they will be cemented into the system.* It becomes very difficult once a new earning level has been established to correct those times. One cannot even completely revise the methods, as a means of proving the need to change the times. The new earning power is acceptable, to the operators at least, and they will believe that management are trying to cut their rates. The anomalies will creep and grow in all directions and lead to 'wages drift'. This will also cause further dissatisfaction amongst other employees who fall behind. There is no end to this.

Control of Wages Drift

There are perhaps three main ways in which management can control this situation, if they have the will.

1   A close eye may be kept on methods and earnings. If a useful change is spotted, it could be authorised, and immediately re-studied. The employees could be given an award, as in the suggestion scheme. Why should they not benefit from their initiative?
2   If the method change is not acceptable, steps should be taken to ensure that the authorised method is used at all times.
3   The incentive scheme can be so designed that earnings above an agreed level cannot be achieved. Graded measured daywork schemes are worth close consideration. Some form of ceiling on earnings must also be examined in close detail, despite some disadvantages.

If no ceiling is stated, management by implication accept that there is no ceiling! Therefore, the employees will aim high.

Standard Times without Control

For companies who choose, as a deliberate policy, to adopt a non-controlled system, the element description is not important. Indeed, for such companies this book will hardly be relevant. The major use for element description in a non-controlled company would be when taking check studies. Check studies are taken during the early part of the job's life, and at the request of the employees. Once the skills *and methods* had improved to the point where the employees could earn 'enough' bonus, the time would become acceptable to them because of its looseness. As it would be policy to accept high earnings, and allow standard times to remain, the element description after that would be virtually useless. Obviously in such a company, and there are many like this, spending too much time on description, and asking managers to authorise the description, would be a waste of time. It is possible to find companies where such a system works quite well. This would be where the product life in general is very short, and times are constantly being withdrawn and replaced. Even in a case like this, the company should consider a sophisticated synthetic data system, and synthesis.

Controlled Standard Times

For those companies that adopt a more controlled situation, not only is element description important, but the authorisation of that description by management is equally vital. It is the major means by which the method can be shown to have changed, and thus the time changed. On the other hand, if the method change is not acceptable to management, the element description can be used to 'retrain' the operators in the original, and thus authorised method. Furthermore, realising that performances of say 110 are really quite high, management would investigate any work showing performances nearing 110, *just to confirm the method*. This does not mean that wages need be low, but at least the data, so widely used throughout the company, is reliable.

Advantages of Sound Element Description

Finally, it is emphasised that a thorough element description is needed when preparing times, *to recognize a qualified operator*. It helps towards a deeper understanding of the method and aids accurate rating. The finer and more precise the detail, aided by methods of timing, the greater the accuracy of element times, and the opportunity to develop synthetic data.

Bearing in mind then that precision of description is governed by the level of accuracy selected, the following list summarises the advantages of using a proper element description instead of the 'rough notes' that are usually called element descriptions.

1   One is able to determine, before and during studies, whether operators are qualified in the method authorised by management.

2   There is a basis for moving towards an agreed level of accuracy with some confidence. This can be included in discussions with trade union representatives, if it is felt useful.

3   The calculations of relaxation allowance, enhancing the specified conditions, can be completed as thoroughly as needed.

4   It is a means of establishing times in a consistent and economic manner. Extra preparation cost is quickly recovered by both tangible and intangible benefits.

5   Provision can be made for the use of work measurement that will yield a sound synthetic data base. Transfer of times and validation is much improved, causing a wider use of the perhaps mis-aligned data bank concept.

6   It is much easier during studies to recognise 'foreign' elements, and deal with them in a logical manner.

7   One is able to determine subsequently whether the job originally described at issue is still being performed. It thus becomes the basis for confirming that change or reverting to the original method.

8   It aids the maintenance and adjustment of times, in an efficient and consistent manner.

9   Greater understanding by everyone should lead to less friction on the shop floor.

10   It releases the brake on some methods improvement, and offers to management and employees a new basis for sharing in productivity improvement, using reduced cost as a base instead of increased output.

Reference has already been made to element types in Chapter Four. In delving a little deeper, an outline of the job to be studied must be considered. To do this an element description, based on a work cycle, is prepared.

B.S. 3138 1979 WORK CYCLE NO. 42001
The sequence of elements which are required to perform a task, or to yield a unit of production. The sequence may sometimes include occasional elements.

B.S. 3138 1979 ELEMENT NO. 42003
A distinct part of an operation, selected for convenience of observation, measurement and analysis.

B.S. 3138 1979 BREAKPOINT NO. 42002
The instant at which one element in a work cycle ends and another begins.

To complete the element description, another few items are used very widely, though not defined:

Title of work cycle	Author
Supportive sketches and	Authorisation of manager
other information	Statement of level of
Element Numbers	accuracy
Element Titles	Dates
Element Types noted	

The Description and the Study

Clearly, to be able to describe a job at all, the pattern of movement involved must first be observed, and any technical details. During the observations, the practitioner must be aware that the purpose of the description in the first instance is the subsequent study of the work cycle using a stopwatch. Hence the moments at which the time is recorded for any element is dependent on the choice of breakpoints. Description can be enhanced by a sketch or a 2-handed process chart.

The Role of the Breakpoint

Breakpoint selection is one of the most critical features in preparing to take a study. Logically quite simple, all one has to do is separate the work cycle into different types of element.

Manual	Machine
Repetitive	Occasional
Constant	Variable

In reality, this is not quite so easy to understand and do as it is to state. There are a number of reasons for this.

1 The element size may prove to be too large or too small.
2 There is a need for breakpoints to match up with one another, in complex cycles.
3 There are other factors not easy to explain.

To assist in overcoming some of these problems, perhaps it is best to offer some examples for closer consideration.

A Simple Case

A very simple case to begin with may involve an operator loading and unloading a machine.

Fig. 21 shows a work cycle containing three elements, one of which is a machine element. They are all of reasonable size, i.e. between 0.10 and 0.30 minutes. All the elements are intended to

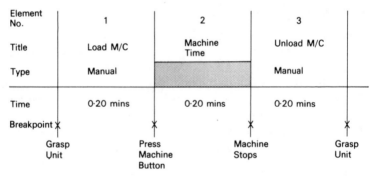

Fig. 21   A very simple work cycle easily studied.

be repetitive and constant. Breakpoints, to begin and end the machine element, are selected as those instants in time which can readily identify the moments at which the machine starts and stops. Element 1 immediately follows the preceding element 3, during a series of work cycles, but not at the beginning. See fig. 22.

Loading a machine is quite different from unloading it, hence the two are separated. There are two logical breakpoints one could choose: either grasp piece (for loading) or release piece (having unloaded it). The point to remember is that *the end of element 3 is in most cases the beginning of element 1*. During any study this pattern must be broken occasionally. For example:

Start breakpoint for element 1
Grasp first piece
or Grasp piece
Finish breakpoint for element 1
Press button
Finish breakpoint for element 2
Machine stops
Finish breakpoint for element 3
Grasp piece
or Release last piece

This is shown clearly in fig. 22.

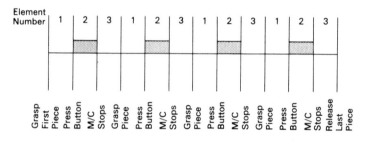

Fig. 22   An over-simplified case of consecutive work cycles (based on fig. 21).

A Modified Simple Case

In the next example, the same cycle will be used, but in this case the machine time will be much shorter. The selection of breakpoint will depend upon the level of accuracy demanded. In a category C study, the machine time may be added to one of the manual elements. Knowledge of precise time for each element *type* is not important. See fig. 23.

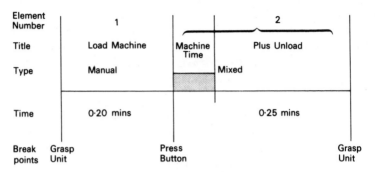

Fig. 23   Element selection on a category C study.

If, on the other hand, the manager had specified category A level of accuracy, the machine time would need to be separated. It would thus be described as a machine element as shown in fig. 24, and a means found to time the elements individually.

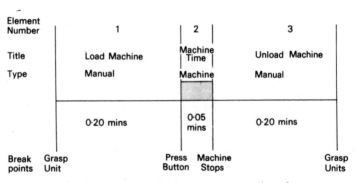

Fig. 24   Element selection on a category A study.

The means to determine these tiny elements has already been developed. The important feature is that the ultimate purpose of the time should decide on level, and thus breakpoint selection, *not the convenience of taking the study*. One further illustration is offered to clarify the concept finally.

A Comprehensive Case Illustration

Take two hypothetical situations in which management at two different companies might choose two different levels of accuracy. In both cases, however, the identical job is to be described.

1   A batch of wood strips is needed, to complete an order. It is decided to cut them on the 'old' circular saw, as the new automatic machine is fully committed. Only 2,000 pieces are needed, and there is no standard time available. There is no specified method, and no case for developing one. The manager decides that a temporary time will be preferable to paying average earnings, and gives the job to one of the established operators. The manager asks work study for a category C time, or temporary time.

2   The circular saw is in regular use with the second company, and requires an operator full time. The method of working is considered quite adequate, and the range of work done fairly average. This is just another routine job. The manager would like a set of times to cover all work done on this machine, and the operator offered bonus. He requests that this be done, and specifies an accuracy level of category B.

In figs. 25 and 26 are shown two element descriptions for essentially the same job, but under these two different circumstances.

A Simulated Study for a Temporary Time

A simulated study for the temporary value is shown in fig. 27. The number of observations or separate studies would be decided by the work study officer, though the manager could request more before issuing the time. The time issued would be clearly identified as such, and would be said to be accurate to ±20%. It would be issued and used only for the 2,000 planks in the batch. It would have been 'economically' prepared, and would be valid and acceptable to both management and employees. There would probably be no requests for check studies, no wish to train the operator, or to reconstruct the

Time Study

COMPANY X	ELEMENT DESCRIPTION SHEET		SHEET 1 of 1
Department Wood Cutting		**Prepared by**	Tony A. Jay
Machine Circular Saw		**Date**	February 20th 1979
Operation Cut plank into three strips		**Checked by**	Mr. D. Manager (Cat. C)
		Date	February 21st 1979
El. No.	**Detail**		**Breakpoint**
1	*Cut off first strip*		GRASP PLANK ◄
	Pick up plank, and place onto machine bed. Push		
	plank towards saw, using the wood guide, and		
	commence the cut. Pick up safety stick, and use to		
	finish the cut. Aside safety stick to bench, pick		
	up and aside first cut piece. Reach for and		
	grasp the remains of the plank.		
			GRASP PLANK
2	*Cut off second strip*		
	Push plank towards saw, using the wood guide, and		
	commence cut. Pick up safety stick and use to		
	finish cut. Aside safety stick to bench, pick up		
	and aside second cut piece. Reach for and grasp		
	the remains of the plank.		
			GRASP PLANK
3	*Cut off third strip*		
	Push plank towards saw, using the wood guide, and		
	commence the cut. Pick up safety stick and use to		
	finish cut. Aside safety stick to bench. Pick up		
	last cut piece, and remaining scrap piece, and		
	place aside to appropriate store. Reach for		
	and grasp next full plank.		
			GRASP PLANK ◄

Fig. 25   Element description for a temporary time.

EI. No.	Detail	Breakpoint
	COMPANY Y	**ELEMENT DESCRIPTION SHEET**	**SHEET** 1 **of** 1

Department	Wood cutting	**Prepared by** Tony A. Jay
Machine	Circular saw No. 87/31	**Date** February 20th 1979
Operation	Cut planks into strips	**Checked by** Mr. W.C. Manager (Cat. B.)
	See attached sheet for layout	**Date** February 24th 1979

EI. No.	Detail	Breakpoint
1	*Load plank to machine bed*	GRASP PLANK
	Pick up plank from store table, lift over safety	
	hood, and lower onto machine bed. Push plank	
	against wood guide and then towards blade, until	
	blade commences cut.	
		BLADE BITES
2	*Cut through length of plank*	
	Push plank firmly through saw, but taking	
	great care. When plank is about 18″ from the end,	
	reach out and grasp the safety stick. Pick up	
	and place the safety stick on end of plank,	
	and use to finish pushing plank through blade.	
		BLADE CLEARS
3	*Aside safety stick and cut piece*	
	Reach for and grasp cut piece, and place aside safety	
	stick to machine bed. Place cut piece into adjacent	
	storage position, turn and reach for and grasp	
	remains of plank. Push plank against wood guide	
	and then towards blade, until blade commences.	
		BLADE BITES
4	*Aside last piece and obtain next plank*	
	Reach for and grasp cut piece, and place safety	
	stick to machine bed. Pick up remaining scrap	
	piece. Place scrap piece into bin, and cut piece	
	into adjacent storage. Reach for and grasp	
	next plank from storage table.	GRASP PLANK

Fig. 26   Element description (category B) for synthetic data.

89

Grasp Plank															
	100	100	100	100											
Cut off 1st strip	35	39	39	37											
	350	390	390	370									1·500	4	0·375
Grasp Plank															
	100	100	100	100											
Cut off 2nd strip	32	30	34	31											
	320	300	340	310									1·270	4	0·318
Grasp Plank															
	100	100	100	100											
Cut off 3rd strip	48	50	47	49											
	480	500	470	490									1·940	4	0·485
Grasp Plank															
															1·178

Fig. 27   Study showing three element times per plank, and four planks cut.

method. Any improvements the operator made as he progressed would be to his own benefit. The temporary time would serve a useful role, and soon become obsolete.

A Simulated Study for Synthetic Data

In the second case, the times need to be more accurate, and more readily altered as future method changes occur. In the meantime, however, a discussion with the manager confirms that the present method is acceptable. Studies are to be taken on the method as observed (but essentially the same method as in the previous case).

The first stage is for the work study officer to show the manager the early notes on how the job is actually seen to be done. Assuming that the description fits what the manager is expecting, more detail is taken. The breakpoints are selected logically by separating different element types from one another. It is recognised that synthetic data is to be prepared, and therefore different sizes of plank and different types of wood have to be incorporated in the studies. A second look at fig. 26 may be helpful here.

Taking Pilot Studies

A pilot study is taken as soon as the manager has given his approval and authorisation to the element description. This may well prove to be decidedly tricky, but no study error is needed, and it is really only an experimental study. It is solely for the benefit of the work study officer, to assist in constructing how the proper studies will be taken. Fig. 28 shows the sort of figures that may emerge.

The pilot study will show that studying to the second description is going to be much trickier than to the first. Indeed, as one

Grasp Plank													
1													
Load plank to M/c Bed	04			05			04				0.13	3	0.04
							FREQ	/PLANK					1/1
Blade bites							TIME	/PLANK					0.04
2													
Cut through plank	29	27	31	27	31	30	30	28	29		2.62	9	0.29
							FREQ	/PLANK					3/1
Blade clears							TIME	/PLANK					0.87
3													
Aside s/s and cut piece	07	08		06	08		08	07			0.44	6	0.07
							FREQ	/PLANK					2/1
Blade bites/clears							TIME	/PLANK					0.14
4													
Aside s/s and last piece		14		12			13			0.39	3	0.13
							FREQ	/PLANK					1/1
Grasp Plank							TIME	/PLANK					0.13
✳	PILOT	STUDY			TOTAL	TIME / PLANK							1.180

Fig. 28 Study showing four element times per plank and three planks cut.

will have to assess rating as well, the task of observing each element *separately* is quite impossible. In fact there need be no problem at all. Using a technique known as differential timing, the studies can be taken as normal, but the element structure and the subsequent analysis allow quite small element times to be established. The objective here is to explain element description, and methods of timing are dealt with in Chapter Seven.

A Comparison of the Two Cases

In the case of category C, perhaps one, two or three studies would be quite adequate. The operator would not need to be fully qualified nor judged to be. After all, management is accepting that method changes will occur, and that there is no time or reason to change the time issued. The life of the time is limited.

In the latter case, it is quite possible that twenty or thirty studies may be needed. The method would be management approved, and the operators of necessity would need to be qualified.

The element times themselves are to be constructed as synthetic data, which requires greater precision, and careful analysis. Management and operators are going to use these times for a long time, and need faith in their accuracy.

Respect for accuracy and consistency is needed by all. It is likely that methods will change as time passes. It is necessary therefore that the times can be checked, and where appropriate corrected to match the newly approved method. The original method upon which the times are based *must be capable of both recognition and reconstruction*. In this way the times are truly controlled by management.

The Delegation of Control by Management

A further study of the two descriptions will show that both use approximately the same number of words, yet the amount of detail of the second description is far superior to the first. This requires skill and experience. It can thus be seen that if relatively inexperienced work study officers are employed, and the full responsibility of establishing times is delegated to them, and *management do not authorise those specified methods*, they will have delegated *control* to someone who is not yet capable of carrying managerial responsibility. It is quite logical to delegate the *preparation* of times to work study, but bordering on the disastrous to delegate preparation *plus* control. As this situation is now very widespread, and traditionally accepted, the only people that can now correct this management flaw are the policy-makers.

The True Value of Sound Management Services Policy

The work of the management services officer is equal in importance and complexity to that of the accountant. The accountant, however, is given a more rigorous training, and is subject to audit. This ensures that his standards are maintained and management have no choice with that profession. In general there is no audit on work study applications, no arithmetic base. Nevertheless it is possible to audit the work of work study. In the mid-1970s an article in the national press stated that 'following an audit into incentive schemes, one department at a large local authority was giving away £300,000 per annum due to poor work measurement'. This may sound impossible, but it is only 20% of 300 men at £5,000 per annum per man. A 20% error is rather more common than many would admit. This labour force might only need three management service officers. When the times given to the accountant are 20% loose, he will still use them as the basis of analysis and control. *What choice does he have?*

To conclude on the role played by element description, it is useful to summarise the major areas of benefit, when this is done well.

1   Greater accuracy of times is possible. Individual analysis of elements based on a better understanding of the patterns of movement helps to ensure that just the right amount of studies are taken. Rating assessment accuracy is improved where it is most important. Allocation of relaxation allowances becomes more reliable.

2 Element times, and thus standard times, become more and more consistent. With management taking a more responsible role, and a wider use of synthetic data, times must be more reliable. Industrial relations are improved.

3 Cost of study is considered against *all* the resources being saved, not simply the savings in labour. In this way, the implications of loose standard times are better appreciated, and pressure to issue the times as rapidly as possible is reduced. It only costs more when it saves even more.

4 The element description is prepared in such a way that it can be used to minimise the number of disputes that normally occur when no one is sure which method was studied.

5 As in P.M.T.S. the detail of patterns of movement are so clear that the description can be used as a significant training aid. Where a job is likely to continue for a long time, as in category A and B work, both work patterns and time taken are clearly defined. It can thus be used even in systematic training schemes.

6 When preparing description at levels A and B, and having to provide greater detail, method improvement possibilities become more obvious, and can be discussed with the manager before study work is commenced.

The Manager Becomes a True Manager

The critical factor always is the level of accuracy chosen by the manager. If the manager asks for a category C time when the circumstances indicate it to be a category A time, the manager should be advised. If, after considering the advice, the manager still authorises a category C time, then the time must be prepared fairly quickly. Element description need not be too thorough, and not many studies need be taken. If there are subsequent problems, it is for the manager to explain why category C was requested. Any manager who allows high performances or unauthorised methods will be precipitating problems, if the time is allowed to remain. *But authorised method can only exist at levels A and B.*

Chapter Seven

Timing

The first point to clarify in this chapter is the difference between time study and timing. Time study is a *total process* of measuring work, primarily by use of a stopwatch, though there are other measuring devices. Time study was defined in the first section of this book. To complete a time study exercise, there are a number of phases to follow. These are shown in fig. 29 and the place of timing is clearly indicated.

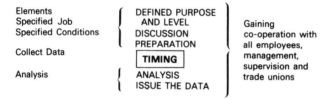

Fig. 29   The six major phases of time study.

The Simplicity of Timing

The actual process of timing, although the central feature of time study, is perhaps the easiest phase of all. With a small amount of training, say two or three weeks, any average person can learn the basis of this limited skill. A little practice, supported by close supervision, and one could soon begin to assist an experienced work study officer. To the uninitiated, it may even seem practical to send an inexperienced trainee to study under their own responsibility. Provided, then, that the study situation seems to be a simple one, with only category C type work, a trainee having just the basic training can produce figures that seem acceptable. Indeed, people like this are widely employed in countless situations throughout the country. They are essentially timing operators, and are not applying time study professionally.

Of course, in order to set about timing, they have to undertake as best they can some if not all of the other phases. In order to learn timing in the first place, they will have had minimum instruction in preparation and analysis. Previous experience in another job and logic will have provided them with some skills in discussion.

This is the approach used by many engineering companies. Production engineers provide the metals cutting and 'methods' base. *They avoid the important responsibility of personally measuring work* by employing 'time study officers'.

The skill of a well qualified work study officer would go much deeper. Firstly, he would have a knowledge and experience of other work measurement techniques, *and may recommend using a technique other than time study*. Secondly, assuming time study was the most effective technique to use, he would also be able to advise on level of accuracy, and study to whichever level the manager selected. He would also complete method study on manual based tasks, which the production engineer may overlook. Clearly, then, an understanding of timing would not be enough for the well run company.

Methods of Timing

Basically, there are four methods of timing that are fully recognised: flyback timing; differential timing; cumulative timing; selective timing. First consider the general definition of timing, and then the four different types of timing.

B.S. 3138 1979 TIMING NO. 41013
The practice of observing and recording by the use of a watch or other device, the time taken to complete each element.

The above definition presupposes that some form of element description has been prepared, and that a subsequent analysis will take place.

B.S. 3138 1979 FLYBACK TIMING NO. 41014
A method in which the hands of the stopwatch are returned to zero at the end of each element, and are allowed to restart, the time for the element being obtained directly.

B.S. 3138 1979 CUMULATIVE TIMING NO. 41015
A method in which the hands of the stopwatch are allowed to continue to move, without returning them to zero at the end of each element, the time for each element being obtained subsequently by subtraction.

B.S. 3138 1979 DIFFERENTIAL TIMING NO. 41016
A method for obtaining the time of one or more small elements. Elements are timed in groups, first including and then excluding each small element, the time for each element being obtained subsequently by subtraction.

B.S. 3138 1979 SELECTIVE TIMING NO. 41017
A method for obtaining the time of an element, in which the hands of the stopwatch are stopped at the end of the selected element without returning them to zero, and allowed to continue to move when the element recurs. The time for the element is subsequently obtained by dividing the total accumulated time by the number of occurrences.

To Understand, One does not Need the Skill of Actual Performance

It would be foolish to suppose that a reader could learn to time something from a book alone. It is like riding a bicycle, driving a car, or learning to swim. Theory is fine, but it is necessary to *experience* the actions, in order to acquire skill in performing them. Consequently, this book does not attempt to explain how the action of timing is performed. Time study practitioners or trainees already know, or will have to learn by practice. For managers, accountants, supervisors and trade unionists, it is the theory and application that is more important. Hence it is assumed that the reader can already time with a stopwatch, is soon to learn, or indeed does not need to time at all.

The factors that can be explained are:

1 when and how different timing methods may be used;
2 the use of rating when timing;
3 the study forms used;
4 the equipment used;
5 the calculation of study error;
6 dealing with foreign elements, contingencies and ineffective time.

Company Policy and Timing Method

Normally when timing one uses either flyback timing or cumulative timing, as decided by company policy. It is quite simply the one or the other. Indeed, when using either flyback or cumulative timing, one could be said to be taking a *normal* time study. As long as the elements are of reasonable duration, one just times the operator naturally. The duration of shorter elements will depend to a large degree on the skill of the work study officer, and the particular job being studied. Times varying from say 0.1 up to 0.3 minutes would be considered reasonable. Strangely enough a large proportion of work cycles can be naturally sub-divided into elements of about that size.

An example of a normal time study is shown in fig. 30. The details illustrated are those taken at the place of study. Further analysis would be made later at a desk.

As stated in the previous chapter, however, when preparing element description, elements should not be chosen just for convenience of study. There are many occasions when the preparation of data requires a more logical basis. The development of synthetic data is a good example. In such a case it is common to prepare the description first, agree it with the manager, and then discover that some of the elements are really too short to study using normal timing methods. The discovery would often be made during a pilot study when times are as low as 0.02 or 0.05. Needless to say, the element description is not changed but the timing method. This is how differential and selective timing methods came to be developed.

Time on 2-17	Eff. Time				Operation: Assemble					Study No. 3/28		
Time off 2-29	Ineff. Time				nuts and bolts					WSE Tony A.JAY		
Elapsed	Time Observed				(see figure 57. for					Date Nov 1st 1979		
TEBS 1·00	Net Elap. Time				element description)							
TEAF 1·10	Actual Error				Rating: B.S.I 0-100					Sheet 1 of 1		
CHECK Time	% Error				Watch: G-miminute/Flyback					Operator Miss Brown		
Grasp Bolts												
	105	100	90	90	100	100	105					
Take and check 2 bolts	26	28	30	27	31	30	29					
Grasp Nut												
	100	100	100	105	95	90	95					
Put nut onto bolt	17	15	15	15	16	19	15					
Grasp Nut												
	100	95	95	105	100	100	100					
Put nut onto bolt	18	16	19	17	15	15	18					
Grasp Bolts												
	95	100	110	95	100	105	95					
Take and check 2 bolts	29	28	26	29	28	31	31					
Grasp Nut												
	110	110	100	100	90	105	100					
Put nut onto bolt	15	14	17	16	19	14	15					
Grasp Nut												
	100	100	90	90	100	105	100					
Put nut onto bolt	17	15	17	19	17	15	17					
Grasp Bolts												
			100				90					
Bolts from tray			31				35					
Grasp Bolts												
or Grasp Nuts												
					95							
Nuts from tray					47							
Grasp Bolts												

N.B Small but really not enough to illustrate points

Fig. 30   A study which is completed but still to be analysed.

Suffice it to say that most companies today have accepted the flyback method of timing as the basis of their time study system, and that if flyback timing can be done cumulative timing is very easy to adopt.

Differential Timing

Differential timing is the first of the two alternative systems that we may consider. This will only be used when the elements selected are too small to study using normal timing. In other words, the work study officer creates this situation when preparing the element description. Before this, the manager can affect things by the level he chooses. It is not something imposed, but a conscious decision made to meet the needs of the job. There is clearly a good reason why these small elements should be timed individually. One *can* 'lose' them, just by adding two elements together and calling it one element! To decide upon logical elements at description stage, and then add them together at the timing stage, just because it seems difficult to time, is bad practice.

An Illustration of Differential Timing

The best way to illustrate differential timing in operation is to consider an example that has already been used. Reference back to figs. 26 and 28 shows a description and a simulated study. The level of accuracy is chosen by the manager as category B, and the method has already been authorised by him. Elements 1 and 3 are rather small. It would be possible to study element 3 as a separate element, but it would require intense concentration.

Look once again at fig. 28. The sequence of elements that occurs with each plank is 1 2 3 2 3 2 4, and it is a very repetitive cycle. Here is a case where the principle of differential timing could be used, but actually using normal timing. All that has to be done is 'time the elements in groups, first including and then excluding each small element'. In the case of cutting up planks above, the elements would be grouped as follows:

1 2 3   2 3   2   4 − 1 2 3   2 3   2   4

Then, as in the definition, 'the time for each element being obtained subsequently by subtraction'.

$$1 \; 2 \; 3 \text{ minus } 2 \; 3 = 1$$
$$\text{and} \quad 2 \; 3 \text{ minus } 2 \;\;\; = 3$$

Fig. 31 shows how the actual times shown in fig. 28 would be studied in practice. This is immediately followed by the analysis of the element times by subtraction. It can be seen that there is a very minor discrepancy, and this has been left in deliberately. Time study can never be absolutely accurate, and dependent upon the days chosen for study so will the time marginally alter. This is a fact of life.

Grasp Plank													
1 + 2 + 3	40	38	42							1·200	3	0·400
Blade bites												
2 + 3	35	39	35							1·090	3	0·363
Blade bites												
2	31	30	29							0·900	3	0·300
Blade clears												
4	14	12	13							0·390	3	0·130
Grasp Plank												
			Element 1	=	0·400	−	0·363			▪	0·037
			Element 2							=	0·300
			Element 3	=	0·363	−	0·300			=	0·063
			Element 4							=	0·130

Fig. 31 Use of the differential method, though employing normal timing.

Element	Pilot Study Times (fig. 28)	Differential Study Times (fig. 31)
1	0.04	0.037
2	0.29	0.300
3	0.07	0.063
4	0.13	0.130

With the pilot study, everything would be happening much too quickly to rate the elements anyway, hence they are not valid. With the study taken as a differential timing basis, there would have been adequate time to rate.

It is clearly possible, then, using differential timing, to take one normal study only each time one takes a study. The secret of this approach is in the preparation of the element description, and the pilot study.

Selective Timing

Selective timing is simply an alternative method of timing to differential. Change the plank being studied from three pieces per plank to two pieces per plank. The pilot study in this case would produce times as shown in fig. 32. These have again been taken directly from fig. 28. The sequence of elements during a study would be as follows:

    1 2 3 2 4 − 1 2 3 2 4 − 1 2 3 2 4 − 1 2 3 2 4

No longer can we combine 1 2 and 3 as above, as there is no 2 3 to subtract. It is possible to have 2 3 combined and 2 separate, but this will leave a tiny element 1 to study somehow. One way is to combine elements 4 1, and selectively time out element 1. The sequence of observations, starting at element 2, would thus be:

    2 3   2   4 1   2 3   2   4 1   2 3   2   4 1

The study times using this particular choice are shown in fig. 33. Once again element 3 is calculated using the differential timing concept, but the time is not known for 1 and 4 separately, only combined. It becomes necessary, therefore, *to take an extra study* using selective timing on the shorter element 1. Once this has been established, the time for element 4 is calculated by subtraction. Finally, in the case of cutting one

Grasp Plank												
	04		05		04							
										0.130	3	0.043

Blade bites												
	29	27	27	31	30	28						
										1.720	6	0.287

Blade clears												
	07		06		08							
										0.210	3	0.070

Blade bites/clears												
		14		12		13						
										0.390	3	0.130

Grasp Plank												

Fig. 32   Pilot study for a plank cut into two strips.

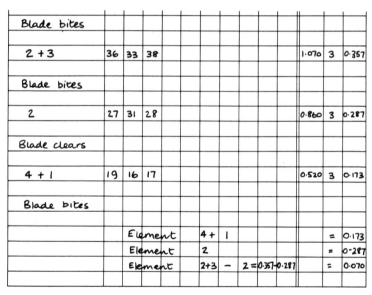

Blade bites												
2 + 3	36	33	38							1.070	3	0.357

Blade bites												
2	27	31	28							0.860	3	0.287

Blade clears												
4 + 1	19	16	17							0.520	3	0.173

Blade bites												
		Element		4 +	1						=	0.173
		Element		2							=	0.287
		Element		2+3	−	2 = 0.357−0.287					=	0.070

Fig. 33   Plank being cut into two strips using normal time study, plus differential timing, but still needing selective timing.

103

piece from a plank, the following sequence of elements would occur:

1 2 4 1 2 4 1 2 4 1 2 4 1 2 4

Here it is clear at once that to study this the following sequence would be selected:

2   4 1   2   4 1   2   4 1

Again, using selective timing, element 1 would be timed separately and element 4 found by subtraction.

Differential Timing with more than one Study

In some books, it is suggested that when establishing times using differential timing, one may have to take studies in pairs, or even more, and then subtract one set of times from the others. In this case, because one needs to take a second study anyway, one can choose between differential and selective. The choice usually lies with the work study officer. A final sequence of elements is offered to illustrate this choice. Element duration as in previous examples.

1 2 3 4 1 2 3 4 1 2 3 4 1 2 3 4 1 2 3 4

Differential timing could be done taking three studies with a different combination of elements each time.

a)	1 2	3 4	1 2	3 4	1 2	3 4	
b)	2	3 4 1	2	3 4 1	2	3 4 1	
c)	1 2 3	4	1 2 3	4	1 2 3	4	

The alternative of selective timing would be done taking again three studies.

a)	1 2	3 4	1 2	3 4	1 2	3 4
b)	1		1		1	
c)		3		3		3

It is only by illustrating examples in this way that one can begin to see that time study can be more complicated than many imagine. Of course, one can always follow the current trend, the easy way out, and employ trainees to give away the company profits.

Small Elements by Analysis

Another method of establishing a time for a small element is during the analysis phase. Assume for a moment that two adjacent elements exist: one is a small constant element, the other is a variable element. These can be studied together and later plotted onto a graph. See fig. 34.

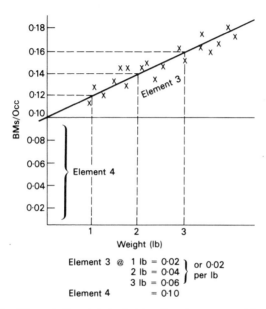

Element 3 @ 1 lb = 0·02 ⎫ or 0·02
          2 lb = 0·04 ⎬ per lb
          3 lb = 0·06 ⎭
Element 4   = 0·10

Fig. 34   Elements 3 and 4 studied together, but separated by analysis.

Selective Timing Isolated Elements

There are occasions when selective timing would be easier to apply than differential timing. When maintaining an existing standard time, it may be that one small element will change. The manager asks for the standard time to be altered. There is no need or basis for changing all the other elements. The method and circumstances are virtually the same. Hence, the new element only is timed, using selective timing, and that one element alone is changed.

105

Rating while Timing

There are times during the timing phase when rating is not always necessary. Taking a pilot study is one example. Establishing data for method study is another. Obviously one tends to rate during any study, but in some cases it is of less importance. Normally when studying, however, each element time that is recorded is also allocated a rating assessment. The actual sequence of events for each element, when using flyback timing, is shown below.

1 At breakpoint, look at watch and observe time.
2 Click watch.
3 Write down rating and time on study sheet.
4 Look back at operator. Check for method. Assess rating. Look for breakpoint.
5 At breakpoint, look at watch and observe time.

Rating is a vague concept that has never been fully resolved. It is quite possible that it never will be. In the meantime one must accept that it is still necessary, and that it is applied during time study as suggested above. There are techniques where the rating factor has been allowed for, such as P.M.T.S.

Forms used when Timing

The forms used when taking time studies are very much the same, whoever designs them. Naturally there are some variations but they are fairly minor. Fig. 30 shows a typical study sheet for use when studying repetitive cycles. Fig. 35 shows how the bottom of this same sheet has been altered for studying non-repetitive work. Normally any company will carry a supply of both types of study sheet.

Few headings are added to either sheet, as they need to be flexible in use. One may take a series of normal studies, or add selectively timed elements to normal studies. Any headings that are necessary to clarify the study would be added by the work study officer during the study, or at the analysis phase.

Time on	Eff. Time			Operation:			Study No.		
Time off	Ineff. Time						WSE		
Elapsed	Time observed						Date		
TEBS	Net Elap. Time								
TEAF	Actual Error			Rating:			Sheet of		
CHECK Time	% Error			Watch:			Operator		

Fig. 35   A time study form, modified to take non-repetitive studies.

Timing Equipment

Generally speaking, the equipment needed to take a study is very basic. A study board specially designed for time study is widely available. Added to the board is a bulldog clip to hold any papers in place, and a stopwatch holding clip. It is not considered that this common piece of equipment requires further explanation.

The stopwatch again is very basic. The only point that needs explanation is that the stopwatch used in time study was specially designed for this work. It is sometimes referred to in the jewellers' profession as a time and motion stopwatch. In other words one cannot use just any stopwatch.

Most time and motion stopwatches today are calibrated in centiminutes rather than seconds. The wind button normally has incorporated in it the flyback mechanism. By sharply depressing this button, and releasing it quickly, the hands of the watch will return to zero, and immediately restart. There is also a second button on the side of the watch. This mechanism simply starts and stops the hands at alternative presses. It is thus used for selective timing.

There are a number of variations built into watches by

107

different manufacturers. One example is the split-hand watch, but it is not very widely used.

No doubt, within the next few years, more and more electronic watches will become available, and they should be easier to use, though the basic principles of timing are unlikely to change for a long time to come.

Some very specialised timing equipment has been developed. The use of these devices, however, is not spreading very rapidly. It is quite possible that they will only ever be used in very special circumstances. One example is the development of a timing device linked to a tape recorder for use in the mining industry. This development only took place because it was so difficult to use the normal stopwatch. A second example is a device developed for the multi-recording of work done by forestry workers.

Generally speaking, it is likely that whenever such devices are used the company would only employ people already skilled in the use of the stopwatch. These devices, therefore, are considered to be outside the scope of this book, which concentrates upon the fundamental base by which work is measured using a stopwatch.

Calculation of Study Error

When taking a time study, it is possible under some circumstances to make errors, without being aware of these errors. This is most likely to occur when using flyback timing, as the watch hand is constantly being returned to zero, to start again. When using flyback timing, therefore, the work study officer has to calculate what is known as study error.

Imagine that you have two stopwatches beside you. They are started at zero simultaneously. One watch, however, is allowed to run for exactly one hour, the other has the flyback button pressed each minute, and each time the button is pressed one minute is recorded on a piece of paper. Of course, at the end of one hour as shown on the first watch, the sixtieth minute on the second watch should just have been observed. If there is a difference something is surely wrong. For a start, either of the two watches, or both, may be inaccurate. Assume they are right. The recorder may have missed a whole minute, or two whole minutes, as a result of distraction. Alternatively there may be a slight reading error on almost every occasion, which accumulates to a significant error. To avoid any of these possibilities, every time a study is taken by a work study officer he is asked to calculate a study error.

It is impossible to study consistently to a zero error, hence a tolerance of percentage error is allowed. The Institute of Management Services recommends that ±2% is reasonable. Outside that, the study should be rejected.

The first stage of calculating study error is to establish the source of the master or known correct time. This can be taken from a special clock at the company, or even the telephone speaking clock. All one needs to start the correct master time is to record the time at the beginning.

This is known as the *time on*. As this time on occurs, one has to co-ordinate the stopwatch with the master clock. This is done by zeroing the watch exactly at the time on. The watch should be wound up and the hand running when this is done.

The second stage is to commence the study. The work study officer waits for the first start breakpoint to occur, and at that instant reads and zeros the watch, and records the time as TEBS, or 'time elapsed before start'. During TEBS, the work study officer can hold any discussions necessary with the operator, supervisor, or anyone.

The third stage is to take the study. Every centiminute that passes must be recorded. For example, someone may talk to the work study officer, and he does not observe the operator. Nevertheless the watch is still running, and the time would be recorded as ineffective.

The fourth stage occurs after returning to the office, or master clock. The last stopwatch time recorded is the time taken from the very last element observed, until a time selected on the master clock is reached. This time is called *time off*. The last time taken from the stopwatch, from the last element breakpoint to the time off, is known as 'time elapsed after finish' (TEAF). The correct time elapsed is found by subtracting time on from time off. An analysis is made of all the watch recorded times, and these are compared to the known master time, or

Time Study

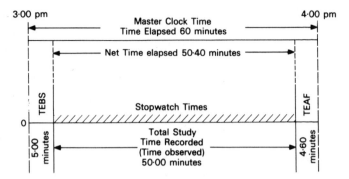

Fig. 36   Comparison of the single master time and all the stopwatch times added together.

time elapsed. See fig. 36 for an illustrated example. One last but important point is that the Institute of Management Services now recommends that TEBS and TEAF are added together and called 'check time', and that this check time is subtracted from the elapsed time before the study error calculation is made. This is called the net elapsed time, and a calculated example is shown in fig. 37.

Time On	3–19 pm	Effective Time	8·59
Time Off	3–30 pm	Ineffective Time	0·00
Elapsed Time	11·00	Time Observed	8·59
TEBS	1·37	Net Elapsed Time	8·51
TEAF	1·12	Study Error	+0·08
Check Time	2·49	% Study Error	+0·94%

Fig. 37   Calculation of study error using the latest recommended procedure.

110

Reasons for Taking Time Studies

There are a number of reasons for and circumstances in which one may be asked to time an operator, or process.

1 A temporary time is needed: check studies.
2 For method study data: validation studies.
3 General information: pilot studies.
4 Studying repetitive work for standard times. Studying non-repetitive work for standard times.

A temporary time would be based on a small number of normal time studies at category C level. This should present no great difficulty.

Check studies and validation studies, using time study, are very similar. They require first that the method of working is checked, to ensure that the method is the one described for the time in question. Secondly, the studies are taken in the same way as the original studies, using the same breakpoints and methods of timing. Sometimes a useful alternative is just to sample working (rated), and not working, *to determine the reasons why bonus is not being earned*, rather than check the accuracy of the element times.

When establishing data for method study, studies need not be too accurate. Much depends upon the circumstances, and it is left to the skill of the work study officer to decide. For example, he may wish to construct a multiple activity chart, for subsequent analysis. In time, this may result in a new method, and the measurement again of the new method to provide standard times.

A pilot study is of necessity an experimental study. It is used to establish, in the mind of the work study officer, how to take the more formal studies. Hence, rating, study error and accuracy are all of less consequence.

The study taken to provide general information for management must be considered in relation to accuracy needed, and any implications for the employees. It may thus be fairly rough, or even very professional. The use to which the data will be put is the deciding factor.

When taking time studies of repetitive work, the major factor involved must be that of level of accuracy required. This has already been adequately covered, and little more need be added. The standard forms used in taking repetitive studies are shown at several points in this book, but the first full example can be restudied in fig. 30.

The study of work that is going to occur over and over again, but is not very repetitive, is a new consideration. To emphasise the type of work in question, think about the job of an electrician doing contract work. His work continues day after day, week after week, yet every job undertaken may be different. Repetition, of course, exists, but this type of job is normally referred to as non-repetitive work. There have been times when this complex task has been considered to be almost impossible to time. Yet today it has been and continues to be measured. Sometimes time study is used as the basic measurement technique.

The problem in timing this work is twofold.

1 Methods of working are invariably inconsistent.
2 The work study officer usually does not know which element sequence to expect.

There is nothing wrong with this; it is the nature of the job, and probably it will never change. The truth has emerged, however, that it is sometimes better to study (albeit inaccurately) rather than not study at all.

There are two major principles that enable one to overcome this difficult area.

1 Recognition of larger elements occurring in changing sequences.
2 The methods by which standard times are prepared and issued.

To study this non-repetitive work, the work study officer uses a slightly different design of study sheet. See fig. 35. Breakpoints and description almost have to be made up as one takes the study, hence some considerable experience and knowledge of the job is necessary. Before moving to non-repetitive studies, officers should be thoroughly experienced in repetitive study work. Data produced from such studies must be extensive, and prepared as synthetic data. Issued standard times are probably best analysed, using techniques such as comparative estimating. Many of the basic elements could be better prepared using P.M.T.S., and so once again we are moving into areas of skill beyond the scope of this book.

Timing the Unexpected

The only major item that now remains is dealing with the unexpected. When taking a study, the work study officer knows in the main what to expect. The element description preparation will cover all those elements that occur reasonably frequently. Anything overlooked by the work study officer may have been spotted by the manager. Nevertheless almost anything can occur. To cover the unexpected, three special categories of work have been established.

1 Contingency.
2 Foreign element.
3 Ineffective time.

The first, contingency, is a valid piece of work or delay that occurred during study but was not included in the description.

The second, any work done by the operator during study which should not have been done, is extracted from the study. It is best to confirm these elements with the manager first. He may wish them to be included as contingencies.

The third, ineffective time, is where any kind of break occurred in the study but was clearly not part of the job. The only reason it is needed at all is to allow calculation of the study error.

Chapter Eight

The Analysis of Time Studies

The analysis of completed time studies discussed in this chapter is limited to the study itself, the element data showing basic minutes per occasion, and the set-up sheet. A number of fairly simple stages are involved.

1 Calculating study error.
2 Calculating basic minutes per occasion.
3 Calculating contingency allowance.
4 Discussing foreign elements with manager.
5 Making up a time study top sheet.
6 Use of the study register.
7 Transferring data to the set-up sheets.
8 Deciding when sufficient studies have been taken.
9 Preparing variable elements.

The study shown earlier in fig. 30 is used to illustrate several of these stages. To calculate study error, several simple calculations have to be made.

Time Elapsed	=	Time Off—Time On
Check Time	=	TEBS+TEAF
Net Elapsed Time	=	Time elapsed—Check Time
Effective Time	=	That portion of the elapsed time, excluding the check time, the worker engage in the proper performance of a prescribed task.
Ineffective Time	=	That portion of the elapsed time, excluding the check time, spent on any activity which is not a specified part of the task.

Time Observed   =   In this book, time observed is taken to be Effective Time + Ineffective Time.

Time observed should not be confused with *observed time*, which measures individual elements.

To calculate study error, all stopwatch recorded times must be considered. In the analysis of the study, therefore, contingency type elements are added into effective time, and foreign elements are added to any recorded ineffective time. It is the total time observed with a stopwatch, excluding TEBS and TEAF, which is compared to the net elapsed time. Hence included in time observed there are elements as described on the element description, foreign elements, contingency elements and ineffective time. Unless all the times observed with the stopwatch are recorded as seen, and subsequently used in the calculation of study error, something will be wrong. In fig. 38 the calculation of study error only is demonstrated.

Calculation of BMs per Occasion

The calculation of basic time for one element is very simple. The formula used for this calculation is:

$$\text{Basic time} = \frac{\substack{\text{Observed time of} \\ \text{one element}} \times \substack{\text{Assessed rating} \\ \text{of that element}}}{100 \text{ (when using B.S. rating scale)}}$$

Two more definitions from British Standard are important here.

B.S. 3138 1979 BASIC TIME NO. 43023
The time for carrying out an element of work, or an operation, at standard rating.

B.S. 3138 1979 OBSERVED TIME NO. 43001
The time taken to perform an element, or an operation obtained by means of direct measurement.

115

Time Study

Time on 2-17	Eff. Time 9·73	Operation: Assemble	Study No. 3/28
Time off 2-29	Ineff. Time —	nuts and bolts	WSE Tony A. JAY
Elapsed 12·00	Time Observed 9·73		Date Nov 1st 1979
TEBS 1-00	Net Elap. Time 9·90		Sheet 1 of 1
TEAF 1-10	Actual Error 0·17	Rating: B.S.I. 0-100	
CHECK Time 2·4	% Error −1·72	Watch: Centiminute Flyback	Operator Miss Brown

									Eff Time		
Grasp Bolts											
	105	100	90	90	100	100	105				
Take and check 2 bolts	26	28	30	27	31	30	29		2·01		
Grasp Nut											
	100	100	100	105	95	90	95				
Put nut onto bolt	17	15	15	15	16	19	15		1·12		
Grasp Nut											
	100	95	95	105	100	100	100				
Put nut onto bolt	18	16	19	17	15	15	18		1·18		
Grasp Bolts											
	95	100	110	95	100	105	95				
Take and check 2 bolts	29	28	26	29	28	31	31		2·02		
Grasp Nut											
	100	100	90	90	100	105	100				
Put nut onto bolt	15	14	17	16	19	14	15		1·10		
Grasp Nut											
	100	100	90	90	100	105	100				
Put nut onto bolt	17	15	17	19	17	15	17		1·17		
Grasp Bolts											
		100			90						
Bolts from tray		31			35				0·66		
Grasp Bolts or Grasp Nuts											
				95							
Nuts from tray				47					0·47		
Grasp Bolts											
						Total Eff Time			9·73		

Fig. 38   Analysis of study error.

Hence, the calculation of basic time for the first element seen in fig. 39 is:

$$\frac{26 \times 105}{100}$$

The 26 in this case equals 26 centiminutes. The next stage will be to convert from centiminutes to minutes, and to three decimal places, so many people miss out the decimal point on the sheet. It is made as a mental note, and is generally understood. Also, to minimise any possibility of error this figure is put in red. Thus, the 273 shown at this first element is in red, and *is understood to be either*:

1   27.3 centiminutes or
2   0.273 minutes

100	90		90
28	30	and	27
becomes 280 (red)	becomes 270 (red)		becomes 243 (red)

The basic time for all common elements are added together, and divided by the number of occasions upon which they were observed, to give the BMs per Occ. See fig. 39 for details. These figures will be transferred to a top sheet.

When taking studies of any operation, much of what is observed will be expected to occur. Inevitably, however, some items will occur that are not fully expected at the time of the study. These unexpected items will fall into one of three categories.

1   Contingency type elements.
2   Foreign elements.
3   Ineffective time.

B.S. 3138 1979 CONTINGENCY ALLOWANCE NO. 43028
A measured or estimated allowance of time, which may be necessary for inclusion in the standard time, to cover specified and legitimate work activities, and/or unavoidable interruptions (not recorded waiting time) in work sequence. Contingency allowance is applied only when it is impractical to treat such items as occasional elements.

Time on 2-17	Eff. Time 9.73	Operation: Assemble	Study No. 3/28
Time off 2-29	Ineff. Time —	nuts and bolts	WSE Tony A. Jay
Elapsed 12.00	Time Observed 9.73		Date Nov 1st 1979
TEBS 1.00	Net Elap. Time 3.90		Sheet 1 of 1
TEAF 1.10	Actual Error 0.17	Rating: B.S.I. 0-100	
CHECK Time 2.16	% Error −1.72	Watch: Continimute Flyback	Operator Miss Brown

	1	2	3	4	5	6	7			Eff Time			
Grasp Bolts													
	105	100	90	90	100	100	105						
Take and check 2 bolts	26	28	30	27	31	30	29			2·01			
	273	280	270	243	310	300	304				1·960	7	0·283
Grasp Nut													
	100	100	100	105	95	90	95						
Put nut onto bolt	17	15	15	15	16	19	15			1·12			
	170	150	150	157	152	171	143						
Grasp Nut											2·264	14	0·162
	100	95	95	105	100	100	100						
Put nut onto bolt	18	16	19	17	15	15	18			1·18			
	180	152	181	178	150	150	180						
Grasp Bolts													
	95	100	110	95	100	105	95						
Take and check 2 bolts	29	28	26	29	28	31	31			2·02			
	276	280	286	276	280	326	294				2·018	7	0·288
Grasp Nut													
	100	100	90	90	100	105	100						
Put nut onto bolt	15	14	17	16	19	14	15			1·10			
	150	140	153	144	190	147	150						
Grasp Nut											2·215	14	0·158
	100	100	90	90	100	105	100						
Put nut onto bolt	17	15	17	19	17	15	17			1·17			
	170	150	153	171	170	157	170						
Grasp Bolts													
		100				90							
Bolts from tray		31				35				0·66			
		310				315					0·625	2	0·313
Grasp Bolts or Grasp Nuts													
				95									
Nuts from tray				47						0·47			
				446							0·446	1	0·446
Grasp Bolts													
									TOTAL Eff Time =	9·73			

Fig. 39   Analysis of BMs per Occasion.

This allowance is made as a percentage addition to the basic times, and is normally added as a once-off calculation, not element by element.

When studying work, certain contingency items will be recognised as an allowable item, and are timed and indicated accordingly. Often seen as a quite separate item in its own right, it is easily timed. On other occasions, it is spotted in the middle of a specified element. Such impure and enlarged elements are circled, and a note made of the inclusion and its cause. It can thus be extracted by subtraction later. See fig. 40. The relationship between repetitive, occasional and contingency elements is shown in fig. 41.

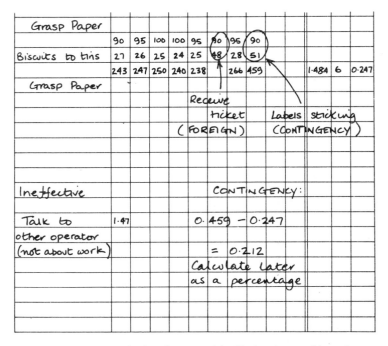

Fig. 40 *Contingency, foreign element and ineffective time, and how these are recorded and analysed.*

Features of an Element	Basis of Element Description		
	Repetitive	Occasional	Contingency
Frequency e.g.	Very Regular 2/1 1/6	Quite Frequent 3/28 5/81	Very Occasional 1/276 1/312
Training opportunity	Easy, and skill development prospects high	Will acquire some skill, but limited	Could be done differently each time
Description	Due to consistent method, it should be easy to describe. It is important to do so	Some variation will occur in practice, so one cannot pin down the description	Just a brief note needed for some kind of identification
Proportion of total Standard Time	Clearly, the cost of the job will *tend* to be governed here	A minor part of cost in many jobs, but can assume large proportions	The cost here is a minor aspect, but it is still important to operators on bonus

Fig. 41   Comparison of the characteristics of contingency elements with those of repetitive and occasional elements.

B.S. 3138 1979 FOREIGN ELEMENT NO. 42009
An element observed during a study which, after analysis is found to be an unnecessary part of the operation.

This is really self-explanatory. It is studied partly for study error and partly for discussion with the manager. If the manager feels it is after all part of the job, it would either be treated as an occasional element, or allocated as part of contingencies. See fig. 40 for example.

B.S. 3138 1979 INEFFECTIVE TIME NO. 43009
That portion of the elapsed time, excluding the check time, spent on any activity which is not a specified part of the task.

As stated in the previous chapter, this is really only needed to be able to calculate study error. It is similar to the foreign element. It is different only because it is known to be nothing to do with the job. There is no need, therefore, to bring it to the attention of the manager. It is better, perhaps, if the manager is not told, and it can simply not be allowed for. It must be clear,

however, that it is not part of the job. If there is any doubt, and
it is a reasonable item to bring to the attention of the manager, it
is recorded as a foreign element. The object here is an industrial
relations matter, and helps to protect the confidence between
employee and the work study officer. Once again this is illustrated in fig. 40.

The Time Study Top Sheet

The 'top sheet' of a time study, as it is usually called, is not a
vital document. It is used mainly because most time studies
extend to more than one study sheet. The top sheet is merely a
summary of all the sheets used up in one study. Occasionally
other information is added to this sheet. It would normally be

WORK STUDY TOP SHEET							
Department Assembly				**STUDY No.** 3/28			
Section Nut and Bolt				**Date** Nov 1st 1979			
Product Nut and Bolt assembly				**W.S.E.** Tony A. Jay			
OPERATION				**Oper's Name** Miss Brown			
Assemble nut and bolt				**Clock No.** 38 – 24 – 38			
				From 2-17 **To** 2-29			
Plant Details Manual				**Elapsed Time** 12-00			
Remarks Category B time Requested				**Estimated Av. Rating** 95-105			
				No. of cycles 14			
El Ref	Element	Total BMs	No. of Occs	BMs/ Occ	Freq		
1	Take and check 2 bolts	4·088	14	0·292	1/2		
2	Put nut onto bolt	4·479	28	0·160	1/1		
3	Bolts from tray	0·625	2	0·313	2/14		
4	Nuts from tray	0·446	1	0·446	1/14		

Fig. 42   The top sheet for analysis summary of one study.

121

stapled together with the other sheets, and of course is the top sheet. It can be useful for the work study manager, or any other reader, to start by looking at the summary of the study, rather than to examine each page first. Once a study has been completely analysed, including its top sheet, a record of it is made in the study register. Then before the study is filed in its allocated place further details are analysed as necessary. See fig. 42 for details.

The Study Register

The study register is normally quite simply a register of studies taken by members of the department. Detail included will vary from company to company, as will the content. Essential basic data would include:

> study reference no.; date taken;
> work study officer; job or other details.

If the manager of a work study department wishes to know who is taking studies, and when, the register will provide that information. If a query is sent through, from management or the unions, regarding details of a study, it can quickly be found.

The Set-up Sheet

Before anyone can normally calculate a standard time with any confidence, a comparison between several studies may be vital. If the level of accuracy requested is category C, then one study may be considered enough, and the temporary time can be calculated direct from the top sheet. When levels A and B are requested, however, a whole series of studies are implicit in that request. Yet how many are needed, and by what criteria can one reach decisions? The major method of assessment is a consideration of the data, study by study, as it is completed. The normal method is to summarise all the studies element by element on what is essentially a summary of all the studies. A popular name for this summary is the set-up sheet.

Before discussing the number of studies to be taken, it is best to consider carefully the data that is available on the set-up sheet. A typical example for a repetitive cycle is shown in fig. 43.

Remarks	Manual task	Study No.	3/28	3/31	3/38	3/43	3/62	3/63	Issue
Bulk of time from repetitive		Date	1/11/79	3/11/79	8/11/79	9/11/79	28/11/79	29/11/79	S.M.V.
elements 1 and 2.		WSE	T.A.J.	T.A.J.	M.R.J.	T.A.J.	T.A.J.	A.W.	
Category B time required.		Operator	E.B.	R.D.	R.T.G.	R.T.G.	R.T.G.	E.B.	
method approved by Mr Smith.		Per							
No.	Element Description								
1	Take and check two bolts	Total BMs	4.088	5.117	3.972	8.802	8.550	7.350	25.105
	(Constant/Rep/Manual)	No. of Occs	14	17	12	27	30	25	86
		BMs/Occ	0.292	0.301	0.331	0.326	0.285	0.294	0.292
2	Put nut onto bolt.	Total BMs	4.479	5.508	4.416	9.720	9.780	8.250	28.017
	(Constant/Rep/Manual)	No. of Occs	28	34	24	54	60	50	172
		BMs/Occ	0.160	0.162	0.184	0.180	0.163	0.165	0.163
3	Bolts from tray	Total BMs	0.625	0.888	0.336	0.900	0.840	1.011	3.264
	(Constant/occasional/Manual)	No. of Occs	2	3	1	3	3	3	11
		BMs/Occ	0.313	0.296	0.336	0.300	0.286	0.337	0.306
		FREQ.	2/28	3/34	1/24	3/64	3/60	3/50	11/172
4	Nuts from tray	Total BMs	0.446	1.032	0.412	1.920	1.383	0.846	3.707
	(Constant/occasional/Manual)	No. of Occs	1	2	1	4	3	2	8
		BMs/Occ	0.446	0.516	0.412	0.480	0.461	0.423	0.463
		FREQ.	1/28	2/34	1/24	4/64	3/60	2/50	8/172

Comments:
(i) Check R.T.G.'s method from Work Study Manager
(ii) Observe a minimum of 50 readings
Check with M.R.J. to see why his values are so different
Discuss retraining with M.R.J.

| Dept. Assembly | Sect. Nut and Bolt | Summary assemble nut and bolt | Date Dec 14th 1979 | Ref. N 487 | Sh. 1 |

Fig. 43 How the set-up is used.

It can be seen that on this sheet only constant elements are used. Variable elements are dealt with later.

As stated earlier a constant element is one that tends to remain constant. It is based on the naturally-occurring Gaussian Curve, and is thus capable of having a standard deviation calculated in each case. Also, if plotted on a graph, it can be made to show its characteristics visually. Many attempts have been made to find a means of identifying when enough studies have been taken, but none are entirely satisfactory. There is no mathematical formula, or indeed magic formula, which can answer this question. This is not to say that none are used, but they can never be totally reliable. The rating factor alone can introduce variations in BMs which are inaccurate and unavoidable.

There are a number of ways in which one can gain confidence in the reliability of the data.

1   Acceptance of levels.
2   Management accepting its responsibility with regard to controlling methods in relation to issued standard times.
3   Understanding the nature of work.
4   Highly trained professional work study officers.

The number of studies taken is linked directly with the confidence one has in the resultant data.

Levels of Accuracy Concept and Studies Needed

In accepting the concept of different levels of accuracy, one immediately accepts that for some jobs only temporary times are issued. The number of studies in this case is minimal. At higher levels of data, not only is the manager responsible for authorising the method, or element description, on which the studies are to be taken, but also the responsibility of ensuring that only authorised methods are used. When asking for studies, particularly at category A, method is covered, adequate training ensured, but also a deep understanding of the job, while observing well qualified operators. Method is thus more precise, rating easier and times automatically more consistent than they would otherwise be.

The work study officer, or team, undertaking the studies on A and B work would be able to judge from experience, and observation of the set-up sheet, when enough studies had been taken. This assumes, as above, that the three levels concept is accepted. Consider two 'constant' type elements:

1   where the time was expected to be very consistent;
2   where the time was expected to be fairly inconsistent.

The consistent element could be one of very high repetition, where there is nothing to cause time variation, other than the speed at which the operator works. Even this would have been allowed for in rating. Assume the operator is highly trained and experienced in performing this element. If the individual basic times were plotted onto a graph one could expect to see the pattern shown in fig. 44.

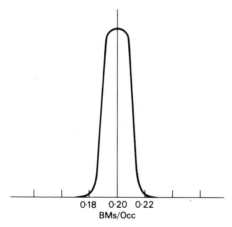

Fig. 44   An acceptable graph for a consistent constant element.

In the second example of an inconsistent constant element, such as walking from house to house when meter reading, the time is bound to vary considerably. There is nothing the management or the operator can do about this. A graph in this case might look like the one in fig. 45. It goes without saying that the nature of work will affect the number of studies needed.

125

Time Study

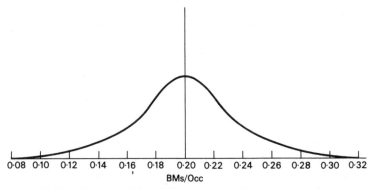

Fig. 45   An acceptable graph for an inconsistent constant element.

Number of Studies Needed when no Policy Exists

Imagine the case where management have not accepted levels of accuracy. Methods are not precisely prepared and agreed. Element descriptions are poorly written. Management do not have the policy of controlling the method to fit the time issued. Indeed methods are allowed to vary. Several studies, each having its own curve, are superimposed on one another. More studies are indicated, but probably not taken. Within months the method has been improved but the time retained. The standard time is already wrong, and the extra studies indicated, even if they had been taken, would have made no difference. Fig. 46 shows the kind of graph one could construct for individual studies, and how they would inevitably combine, on the set-up sheet. Why waste too much money on taking more studies, if there is no sound management policy on time study?

Number of Studies under Sound Policy

The number of studies question can only ever be resolved by sound management policy and training, supported by skilled work study officers. Together, they can soon decide when enough studies have been taken, by a reasoned analysis. Together, they can begin to ensure that graphs look like the ones in fig. 47, and stay that way.

126

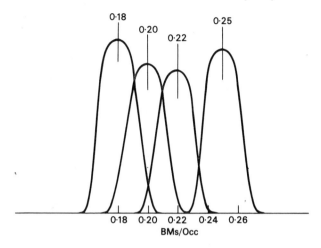

Fig. 46 Four studies taken on a theoretically consistent constant element, but without management control over method.

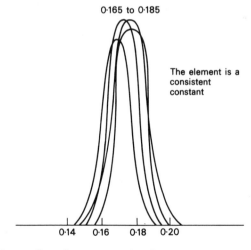

Fig. 47 Four studies taken on a sound method, qualified operators and skilled work study officer.

The same principle applies to variable elements. The difference is the degree of scatter on a graph, instead of the standard deviation.

The Analysis of Variable Elements

The analysis of variable elements can be quite interesting, and great care is often necessary.

B.S. 3138 1979 VARIABLE ELEMENT NO. 42005
An element for which the basic time varies in relation to some characteristic(s) of the product, equipment or process, e.g. weight, dimensions, quality etc.

When preparing a once-off category C type time, one probably would not use such elements. After all the job in question would only be one job, and there would be no comparison of weight, dimension or quality that could be made. Variable elements are normally used when preparing synthetic data. Reference back to fig. 24 will show that the machine element has been isolated. This is because all sorts of sizes and types of wood are cut on this machine. The object is to describe the cutting operation *just once*, but to relate the different times that result from different sizes and types of wood. Hence, a series of studies are taken, and the variable elements analysed study by study. They are even analysed to the set-up sheet, but not totalled. Information about the product is gathered at the time of the study, and the data transferred to a graph. The selection of characteristic is not always as easy as it seems, and the times obtained are plotted against several different characteristics. Usually a consistent pattern can soon be detected. The example of cutting wood plotted on a graph is shown in fig. 48.

Case History of Variable Elements

On one occasion, to quote a case history, a graph was drawn showing a reasonable pattern. After much discussion, and the application of logic to what one would expect, the graph was redrawn. The hurried version is shown in fig. 49, and the revised version shown in fig. 50. The lesson to be learned from

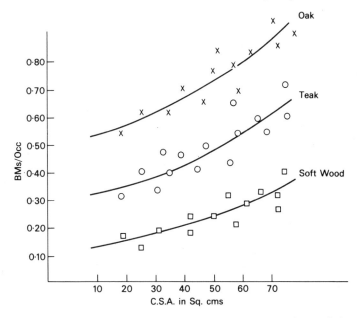

Fig. 48   BMs per Occasion for cut wood taken from the set-up sheet and plotted on the graph.

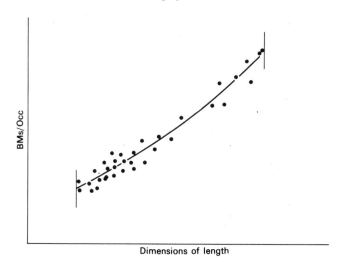

Fig. 49   A line drawn from some variable element data.

129

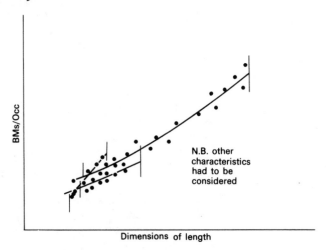

Fig. 50   Three lines drawn for the same data as given in fig. 49. Clearly, some problems were avoided by this revision.

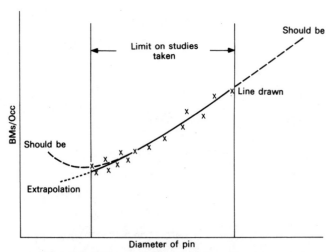

Fig. 51   Why extrapolation can be quite wrong.

this is that one should not easily accept what appears to be a good fit.

Other examples are given in fig. 51 and 52, and these emphasise the need to restrict data to the limits seen by study. Extrapolation beyond the study points will often give an incorrect answer. Variable times are taken from the graph, not direct from the studies. Sometimes, the need to take more variable element times overrules the constant element rule.

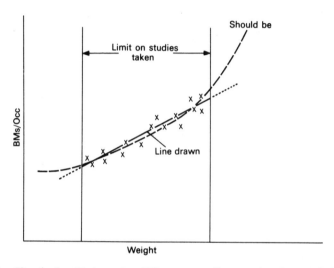

Fig. 52   As fig. 51, but using different naturally occurring characteristics.

Chapter Nine

Frequencies

Frequency plays a logical and very critical role in the further analysis of completed time studies. With a little care and thought, the selection of frequencies need not be a problem. It must be recognised, however, that mistakes can be and are often made, and the effect on the standard times may be significant.

One known error involved putting $\frac{2}{1}$ instead of $\frac{1}{2}$. The financial cost of this one error could have been over £20,000 per annum. Fortunately it was spotted and corrected, ironically, owing to a check study requested by the employees.

Meanwhile, despite the logical base, frequency errors continue to be a major cause of failure for students taking time study practical examinations.

The Need for Frequency

Frequency is needed because the rate of occurrence of elements when taking a time study often does not match the unit of output for which the time is needed.

Take a simple case to begin with, *where a time is needed for one tin*. During the study, the operator picks up two tins at a time in one particular element. It is impossible to time each tin separately. If one assumes the time for this *element* is 0.2 BMs per occasion, the time *per tin* is found as shown in fig. 53.

To illustrate in a more complex way the role of frequency, the two examples used in explaining element description are used once again. One job was used, though two different element descriptions were illustrated for two levels of accuracy. A change in description and breakpoints automatically produces a different set of frequencies, *yet the same time*. These earlier

BMs/Occ	Freq/Tin	BMs/Tin
0·200	1/2	0·100
(The time to complete the element)	(Element occurs once in two tins)	(The time is calculated per unit of output)

Fig. 53   A simple example of the role of frequency.

examples were shown and discussed in figs. 25 and 26. The frequencies for these two studies are shown in fig. 54, where a time is required *per plank*.

Category C Example	A time is required per *plank*		
	BMs/Occ	Freq/plank	BMs/plank
Element 1 Cut off first strip	0·380	1/1	0·380
Element 2 Cut off second strip	0·320	1/1	0·320
Element 3 Cut off third strip	0·480	1/1	0·480
			1·180

Category B Example	A time is required per *plank*		
	BMs/Occ	Freq/plank	BMs/Plank
Element 1 Load plank to M/c bed	0·040	1/1	0·040
Element 2 Cut through plank	0·290	3/1	0·870
Element 3 Aside safety stick and piece	0·070	2/1	0·140
Element 4 Aside last piece	0·130	1/1	0·130
			1·180

Fig. 54   Comparison of the same job, studied at two different levels.

Imagine next that the pieces cut from each plank are going to be used to make up a box. There are three pieces cut from each plank, and four pieces used to make up one box. Management have requested in this new example a time per box, instead of a time per plank.

The basis of taking the time study would not change to fit this alternative unit of output. It is the *frequency* that is used to make

133

the same study fit the new unit of output. Compare the category B example shown in fig. 54 with the example in fig. 55.

Category B Example	A time is required per *box*		
	BMs/Occ	Freq/box	BMs/box
Element 1 Load plank to M/c bed	0·040	4/3	0·053
Element 2 Cut through plank	0·290	4/1	1·160
Element 3 Aside safety stick and piece	0·070	8/3	0·187
Element 4 Aside last piece	0·130	4/3	0·173
			1·573

Fig. 55 Frequencies in this example should be compared with those in fig. 54 (category B example).

The Logic of Frequency

Therefore, it should be clear that *the logic of study* is determined by:

1 the accuracy level demanded by management;
2 the nature of work for the job to be studied;

whereas *the frequency calculated for each element* is determined by:

1 the elements selected for study;
2 the unit of output for which management need a time.

Frequency is defined as follows: *the number of occurrences of an element, per the selected unit of output.* (N.B. The element referred to in this definition is the element as described in the element description.)

Frequencies for repetitive elements can be determined using logic. The frequencies for occasional elements, on the other hand, are calculated from studies taken, or observation. The following examples may help to clarify this point.

Some repetitive frequencies		*Some occasional frequencies*	
2/1	1/1	1/34	4/96
3/4	3/2	2/17	14/135

Frequencies for Occasional Elements

In the three examples of frequency calculation already shown, only repetitive elements have been used. To develop the understanding further, an occasional element is added. To do this, certain information is assumed to be available.

Change the saw blade – Average BMs/Occ = 2.62

Three studies were taken to establish this data, using the original example of cutting planks.

During study A, the saw blade was changed twice, and 81 planks were cut.

During study B, 38 planks were cut, but no change blade observed.

During study C, the saw blade was changed three times, and 93 planks were cut. Frequencies could be established in several ways. If a time was required per plank:

Frequency for change saw blade = 5/212

If a time was required per box:

Frequency for change saw blade = 5/212 × 4/3 = 20/636 or 5/159

The layout and analysis of this occasional element, using two different 'units of output', is shown in fig. 56.

BMs/plank				BMs/Box		
BMs/Occ	Freq./plank	BMs/plank	or	BMs/Occ	Freq/box	BMs/box
2·620	5/212	0·062		2·620	5/159	0·082

Fig. 56   The two frequencies shown are determined by management selection of the unit of output.

One Final Example

To allow an even greater emphasis, an entirely different example is selected. This is not to cover new aspects, but to allow a further consideration of the basic logic. The example to be discussed is based on the element description shown in fig. 57. Some hypothetical figures representing several studies are shown in fig. 58. They are related to the element description just given.

The frequencies for the repetitive elements are quite logical, and are clear even before the study is taken. The frequency of the occasional elements, however, will be determined by the number of bolts or washers selected in the average handful. The majority of time taken to complete the full cycle is covered by the repetitive elements, though the occasional elements are not insignificant. The number of cycles seen per study must be enough to obtain a fair frequency for those occasional elements. To have 'sound' BMs per occasion does not necessarily provide a sound frequency.

When the repetitive element times are clearly dominant, the accuracy of frequency of occasional elements need not be too high. When the occasional element times are clearly dominant, frequency of these elements becomes more critical.

Once again, the concept of level of accuracy arises. For category A standards, one needs to see extra cycles of work. This will give both more reliable BMs/Occasion, and more reliable frequencies. On the other hand, for category C times, less studies are quite acceptable.

Frequencies Controlled by Management

To finalise this chapter, there is still one more consideration. In the example of changing saw blades, all the examples assume the saw blade is reducing in relation to the cuts made. This would occur where the blade was of the 'abrasive wheel' type. The number of cuts that are made in relation to a 'unit of output', or the rate of reduction of the blade due to the material resistance, will determine the frequency of change. Hence, frequency is found by observation, and built into the time.

A quite different situation would occur where the blade is changed perhaps for planning reasons. Assume it is a necessary part of the process to change from a fine-tooth blade to a course-tooth blade. Here the frequency is not related to the unit of output in the same way. It may be that the blade is only

No.	Element Detail	Breakpoint
1	*Take and check two bolts (Repetitive)* Pick up two bolts from stack, inspect one and place on bench. Inspect second bolt and place on bench with left hand and hold. Reach for and grasp nut with right hand.	Grasp Bolts Grasp Nut
2	*Put nut onto bolt (Repetitive)* Pick up one nut and carry to bolt. Hold bolt firm with left hand, and feel nut catching thread. Turn nut three to four times, and then place aside in tray. Reach for and grasp next nut or bolts.　　　　or	 Grasp Nut(s) Grasp Bolts
3	*Bolts from tray (Occasional)* Reach into tray and select a handful of bolts, then place on work surface. Reach for and grasp two bolts.	 Grasp Bolts
4	*Nuts from tray (Occasional)* Reach into tray and select a handful of nuts, and then place on work surface. Reach for and grasp two bolts.	Grasp Nuts Grasp Bolts

Fig. 57　The basis of the final frequency example.

Element No.		Set-up details (Figure 43)	Frequency per Box of 12	Frequency per One assembly
1	Total BMs	25.105		
	No. of Occs	86		
	BMs/Occ	0.292	6/box	1/2 assy's
2	Total BMs	28.017		
	No. of Occs	172		
	BMs/Occ	0.163	12/1	1/1
3	Total BMs	3.364		
	No. of Occs	11		
	BMs/Occ	0.306	110/143	11/172
4	Total BMs	3.707		
	No. of Occs	8		
	BMs/Occ	0.463	80/143	8/172

Fig. 58　Some frequencies related to the set-up sheet shown in fig. 43.

137

partly used for one batch of units, and needs to be stored for future use. One can simply issue an independent standard time for 'Change Wheel' only, and this is claimed for every time management authorises a wheel change. The frequency is thus simplified to a 1/1 basis for most of its elements.

Chapter Ten

Relaxation Allowances

The concept of relaxation allowance is one of the most comprehensive and far-reaching aspects of management in all areas. It is probably true to say that it rarely receives the recognition it deserves. In Chapter Three it was explained that 'work' consists in reality of both work and rest. In Chapter One, reference was made to the experience of Taylor in relation to organised rest breaks. Also in Chapter One comment was made concerning the effect of the economy of a 1% improvement. Recovering from fatigue, plus taking personal needs, usually varies between 12% ɛ ⅃ 20%. This relaxation takes place in one form or another in ˑll work.

The normal understanding of the manager, and the work study practitioner, is quite limited. It tends to be restricted to *only allowing for rest* when preparing standard times or other work measurement based data. Indeed the very definition encourages this view.

B.S. 3139 1979 RELAXATION ALLOWANCE NO. 43025
An addition to the basic time to provide a qualified worker with a general opportunity to:
a) recover from the effort of carrying out specified work under specified conditions (fatigue allowance);
b) allow attention to personal needs; and
c) (rarely) recover from adverse environmental conditions.
The amount of the allowance will depend on the nature of the work, and may be taken away from the place of work under management direction.
Note: Health and Safety Legislation and codes are relevant.

The real implications, however, are much deeper than the definition suggests. Relaxation allowance could quite easily

139

demand a book on its own. It is hoped here to extend any knowledge the reader already has, and to precipitate even further interest and study. Much work has been done in the development of knowledge on the subject, but the understanding and dissemination of information still has some way to go. World-wide research into space exploration has given a considerable boost to this knowledge, and it is very slowly being matched in both commercial and industrial applications.

Link between Relaxation and Ergonomics

Relaxation is now more widely accepted as a sub-division of ergonomics. This is the relatively new science concerned with the human being at work. It considers the study of fatigue, the design of work patterns, the design of machine controls, and indeed the environment. All managers and management services practitioners should have a thorough appreciation of ergonomics.

It may be useful at this stage to express a very much simplified view, thus assisting the reader in identifying the two concepts.

1 Ergonomics may be said to be primarily concerned with reducing fatigue to a minimum or optimum level.
2 Relaxation allowance is rather more concerned with recognising, measuring, and making provision for the fatigue that remains as an inherent component of the job.

Combining these two concepts, four consecutive and fundamental stages of importance can be identified.

RECOGNITION   – The initial realisation and assessment of fatigue causes.
MINIMISATION – The reduction or minimisation of the causes of fatigue.
ALLOWANCES   – The official recognition of recovery from fatigue and personal needs, by allocating allowances as part of the standard unit of work.

RECOVERY   – The method of recovery from the fatigue, and the circumstances involved.

The body, in its normal day to day functions, is a cleverly balanced unit. Fatigue is taking place continuously, yet so is energy replacement. In order to maintain a relative continuity of effort, the natural functions of the body includes, indeed requires, a period of sleep every 24 hours. When sleeping, the body needs to twist and turn to avoid the fatigue of lying still. When not sleeping, the body requires periodic changes in body movement to rest, or to take up relaxed postures. There is no choice; the body demands this to avoid physical pain.

An Illustration of Fatigue

The time scale is vastly different, but one could compare the human being to a car battery. Energy is being both formed and used when the car is running. Sometimes the energy used is greater than the energy formed, and thus the battery needs recharging. Failure to do so will cause the battery itself to fail. The same thing occurs in a human being.

To understand *the nature* of fatigue in the human being, let us consider two situations in which no 'work' is being done.

1   A person could just be watching television.
2   On another occasion this same person could be playing a round of golf.

In both cases, fatigue will be building up in the body, as a result of performing these 'activities'. The fact that the person is not being *employed* does not prevent fatigue building up. Hence, because of this fatigue, the body needs some system of recovery, or energy replacement, in order that the activity can continue.

In the first of the two examples above, the person watching television is able to relieve fatigue by moving, stretching, or even getting up to make a cup of tea. Indeed, anything will do that causes movement, as sitting still can be very tiring. It is quite possibly a factor in selecting channels. Watching BBC all evening can be more tiring than watching ITV, as a change in the level of concentration takes place during the commercial breaks. When watching television, the viewer has a choice of withdrawal at any time, and can thus watch television most of the day without discomfort. Try insisting that someone watches the television on a continuous basis, hour after hour, and expect complaints.

In the second example, the player of golf is performing a series of fairly repetitive movements. Teeing up, hitting the ball (with any luck) and putting away the clubs are obvious examples. There is a certain amount of control over the duration of the game, in a sense that the average golfer will complete eighteen holes in accordance with an accepted set of rules and etiquette. The player will be expected, by the courtesy of the game, to keep moving until the round is completed. Fatigue will build up with only a limited opportunity to recover.

In the round of golf, then, we see a cycle of activity in which fatigue is building up, but at the same time fatigue recovery is also taking place. Like the time spent in bed, it is necessary to move in order to rest. Nevertheless, for any golfer, fatigue build-up will eventually exceed fatigue recovery. After a period, therefore, a differently structured and longer period of fatigue recovery is necessary. This would normally take place after about eighteen holes, and is almost certainly the factor that determines the size of the average golf course. Naturally eighteen holes are now internationally accepted, but it cannot always have been so. Fatigue recovery after a round of golf may include any combination of the following items: sitting down in changing room; having a shower; having a short nap; relaxing in the bar; enjoying a light meal.

As golf is a leisure activity, the golfer has a certain amount of choice in how the final balance in fatigue recovery is taken, but not when. The round must be completed first. It may well be that some golfers would like to continue by going round again, but it is a very fit person who can do so without taking a break. For those readers who do not know the game very well, a round of golf will take about three to three and a half hours.

Once a person has seen enough television, or had enough golf, and has rested for a period that satisfies him, he will proceed to the next activity in his life. Thus one can say that life is just a series of activities, such as watching television, playing golf, gardening, going to work, dancing, and that throughout our life, whether engaged in work, leisure, or even sleep, we need to keep changing our body postures in order that we can continue life. To stop totally motionless for long means that we will suffer extreme pain.

Fatigue at Work

The employee at work is not really different from the person at home. Both combine activity with rest pauses, and both actually want, even need, to engage in activity. The employee, however, accepts in the main that the employer should decide what the activities are, and is prepared to work within agreed parameters. These include methods, quality, safety, targets, procedures etc. Accepting that there is a reasonable will to work under direction, one must also accept that fatigue will build up as previously described. It is clear then that employers must recognise fatigue, and make provision for employees to recover from its effects.

To understand fatigue, and to reduce the causes, is good for business, good for the employees, and good for the country. There are light jobs where the nature of the work is so variable that fatigue build-up is almost matched by fatigue recovery. This can be achieved where the performance of one activity is itself a means of recovering from fatigue. To appreciate this fully, watching television must be considered as an activity. To recover from the fatigue of sitting down, a person gets up and walks around.

Take a manager as an example. He may be able to recover from a physical effort by attending a meeting or making a telephone call. If he has been sitting for a long time and is feeling a little hot, he can go along to the planning office, or across to the warehouse, maybe going into the fresh air. The stroll will be partly restful. In many cases he will drink his tea whilst reading letters, or dictating a memo. Managers can keep going, and only begin to feel exhausted towards the end of the day. The fatigue is not concentrated in one set of muscles, but is spread throughout the body. Hence, the psychology and nature of their work means that few stop and take a rest. This is perhaps the very reason why some managers find it difficult to accept that their employees cannot work without rest pauses, although tea breaks are well established as necessary.

Employees usually do not have the same flexibility, and opportunity, to 'rest by selective activity' that the manager enjoys. It is the continuous use of the same work pattern that can cause excessive fatigue in one set of muscles, or in a particular part of the body. It is rare for the whole body to require rest; normally, it is just the area that is using up the most energy that makes the demands. Often, in the pursuit of improving productivity, management designs the job so that the work is very repetitive. In these circumstances, fatigue build-up will exceed fatigue recovery very quickly in a small part of the body. One way or another, rest will be taken, as there is eventually no alternative that the operator can choose. Even under the threat of a whip, there would come a point when the pain in the muscles became greater than that of the whip lash. Of course, we no longer use the whip as a motivator, but it is a fact that emphasises this important point. Job enlargement and job enrichment are new approaches that recognise and set out to minimise fatigue, or more accurately allow fatigue recovery to take place while working.

Relaxation Recognised

The allocation of relaxation allowance is both an official and a human means of recognising this concept. The employee is thus entitled, indeed expected, to take changes in activity, or to stop performing the defined job, just to ensure that he can later continue. British Standards have now included this concept in the standard unit of work. This is illustrated in a very simple form in fig. 59. The work part includes contingencies.

Let us consider for a moment a hypothetical extension of the above situation. Assume an operator agrees to work at a 100 rating, as best he is able to judge, while working during a normal period. In order to maintain this rate of working, he is asked to stop altogether, rather than slow down, or change the approved work pattern. The pattern of work and rest on the

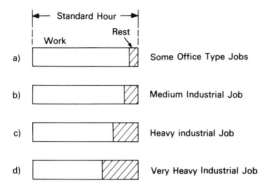

Fig. 59   The proportion of work to rest varies with the job, but rest is a part of any work cycle.

light job may look like the illustration in fig. 60. Note the stability of rating.

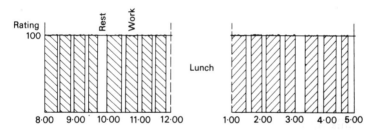

Fig. 60   An operator willing to work at a constrained 100 B.S.I. rating.

In practice, on a normal working day, the normal pattern of working might look more like the example shown in fig. 61. In actual fact, rest pauses would be smaller and more frequent, but it is difficult to draw in at this scale.

The same operator, if asked once again to work under the experimental conditions of stable rating, but on a more physically demanding job, might produce a pattern of work as shown in fig. 62. Compare this to fig. 60. The larger periods of rest are necessitated by the heavier fatigue inherent in the job.

145

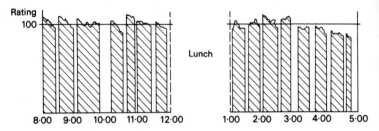

Fig. 61   The more common variation in rating achievement while working.

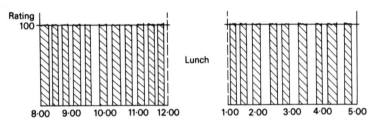

Fig. 62   An operator constrained to work at 100 B.S.I. rating but on a heavy type cycle of work.

Fatigue Related to Performance

In theory, a qualified operator who performs a defined method of work at an average rating of 100 B.S.I. whilst working, takes the evaluated and authorised rest periods and records all details accurately should work at a 100 performance. This would, of course, be based on standard times.

There are, however, a number of other factors which can effect the calculated performance. The major ones are as follows.

1   The accuracy of the issued standard times.
2   The accuracy of the allocated relaxation allowance.
3   The work content itself may vary for several reasons.
4   The number of rejects may vary.
5   Materials may vary from specification.

It should be noted, therefore, that relaxation allowance is only one of the reasons why standard times, and thus performances, are sometimes recognised as being incorrect.

146

The Causes of Fatigue

There are a number of reasons why fatigue may be caused, and these are shown in the form of a diagram, relating energy replacement to fatigue build-up. This is shown in fig. 63. When undertaking any continuous activity, it is necessary to reduce the causes of fatigue, in order that energy replacement can come back into balance.

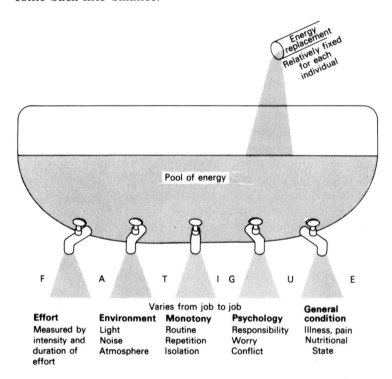

		Varies from job to job		General
Effort	**Environment**	**Monotony**	**Psychology**	**condition**
Measured by	Light	Routine	Responsibility	Illness, pain
intensity and	Noise	Repetition	Worry	Nutritional
duration of	Atmosphere	Isolation	Conflict	State
effort				

Fig. 63   From time to time, fatigue build-up (energy loss) must be allowed to slow down to match energy replacement.

Effort and environmental causes of fatigue tend to require 'immediate' recovery. Hence, one starts and stops work as seems appropriate.

Psychological factors and monotony are independent fatigue

147

causes and tend to build up over a period of months. They are in effect transferred forward day by day.

The general physical condition of an employee is rather more difficult to pin down. It can vary from one person to another quite considerably, and is often beyond the responsibility of the employer.

If one wishes to look at the total concept of work and rest, and it is valuable to do so, an even wider consideration must be given.

Four Aspects of Fatigue

There are perhaps four different aspects to consider, which combine into one comprehensive and complex situation. No order of priority is intended:

> the JOB
> the PERSON
> the ENVIRONMENT
> the PAYMENT SYSTEM

The implications of rest caused by the payment system are slightly different to those caused by the first three. There are reasons, however, why it is felt to be significant in this context, and is thus included.

The job

The design of the job, and the tasks within the job, are clearly of great significance. The methods of working should always consider the causes of fatigue, and how fatigue recovery takes place, in order that an optimum balance can be achieved. Minor variances in the work pattern should be permitted, for if one were to demand precise repetition it would not only mean that extra training time would be required, but also that fatigue build-up would be more intense. On the other hand, one must still establish a basic method of working, in order that some control is exercised over method. Employees have been known to introduce a number of modifications to a basic method, and some small approved modifications need not be beyond the skill of management.

The person
Everyone has different inherent skills, intelligence, strength, and interests. Clearly all people are suited to some types of work more than others. A person who is 'qualified' is defined as having the necessary physical and mental attributes for the job, plus adequate training. An important feature of the working situation is that the employee is suitable for the work he is employed to do. Hence the person is usually selected to suit the work. The nature of the work then becomes a little less relevant. In ergonomics the concept is to fit the task to the person, yet one selects the right sort of person first! The person should then be trained, and where it is judged to be an advantage motivated by features over and above the motivation of the work itself. For example a joiner may be entirely fascinated by his work, but bonus, job security and good communications are extra means by which he may be motivated. Wherever practical, the employee should be offered the opportunity for personal development, for additional, alternative, or more advanced work. This would include upgrading or promotion. All these things represent change from what could become a standard routine.

Those not really qualified for a job, i.e. poorly selected or poorly trained, may suffer a greater fatigue build-up than their more qualified colleagues.

The environment
It has been clearly established scientifically that poor environmental factors, can and do have an adverse effect on a person's ability or willingness to work well. The environmental aspects should be measured and compared to the norm for the type of work under consideration. Information on this aspect is given in some detail in most books on ergonomics, and is gradually being introduced into the legislation on employment.

Where the environment is shown to be inferior to the working requirement, an assessment should be made as to the cost of raising the environmental standard. This cost can then be compared to the benefits to be gained by making the improvement. Where benefit is greater than cost, there should be no problem in reaching a decision. Where benefits are intangible, or clearly less than cost, more consideration is needed. In this field, the analysis of benefit is by no means easy. A greater understanding of relaxation allowances is a great help. If, for example, it is felt that relaxation allowance is an essential under certain conditions, which are quantifiable, then in improving those conditions there must be a case for reducing the allowance. It is natural that employees will feel that their beloved rates are being cut. Once again it must be emphasised that the reason for changing times should be to retain agreed targets, and that earnings opportunity is the same for all. Other means should be found to optimise earnings. To use inaccurate times is illogical, and *in the longer term* is against the interest of the unions and the employees. Hence, if conditions are changed, standards should also be changed.

In addition to reducing the amount of fatigue suffered by the employees, other intangible benefits may include: reduction in strikes (if there are any); greater co-operation; reduced absenteeism; reduced turnover.

The important point is that if the environment is to remain poor a proper allowance must be made for the fatigue that will result from that environment.

In conclusion, when improving the environment, one should not need to be too precise on the cost/benefit aspect. From the human point of view, if the over-all benefit of a project is high, why not allocate some of that benefit to improving conditions without attempting to justify the improvement separately. In this way there would be a net gain quantified for the company, and a welcome environmental improvement for the employees. See fig. 64 for a comparison of two proposals.

It is quite clear that both proposals would be acceptable to any management. The second one, however, could well be much more acceptable to the employees, as they will feel they are sharing in the benefits of change, which of course they are. If one was to analyse carefully the cost/benefit of the environmental change in isolation, it may well be decided not to do it, but at what cost? The intangibles will have been overlooked. Management should always consider adding environmental improvements to any other project, even if they are not included in the proposals. What better time is there to

A project retaining the same environment		The same project but environment improved	
Cost	Benefit	Cost	Benefit
£5,000	£5,000	£7,000	£5,260
once	p.a.	once	p.a.
Pay back in 1 year		Pay back in 1 year and 4 months	

Fig. 64   A project evaluation, with and without environmental improvements.

spend money on intangible benefits than when change is being made, and money is being saved?

The payment system
The major reason that any of us go to work is for money. Naturally, this may not apply to everyone, and of course there are other factors as well, but it is a reasonable statement to make. Much is said about motivation and the various means by which it can be improved, but few writers agree on the subject totally. One researcher will show the benefits of taking certain measures; another researcher will later show that the opposite is true.

All would probably agree that money alone is not the sole means of motivating anyone to give up their own time and be prepared to 'work' for someone else, but that it is a powerful factor. Nevertheless, money is the supreme barter system, and the more of it we have the *wider the choice we have on how to spend our lives*. It thus cannot be ignored as a major motivational factor.

One often reads that, when we earn enough money, then money becomes less relevant. Other factors such as status, job satisfaction and conditions are the new primary factors. Yet who amongst us already earns 'enough'? Who, given twice the money they now earn, would not change their lifestyle at all, but would simply leave the surplus in the bank, or even give it away? One suspects that most people, including managers,

151

accountants, executives even, do not earn quite as much as they would like. How much more might some lower paid employees like? Hence, the amount of money and the system of payment is still very significant.

When the system of payment is linked to output, as it is in many financial bonus schemes, the amount of output and the pace of working come into the picture. As the pace of working for any job increases, so too can the rate of fatigue build-up, and the need to rest. In the same way, an executive under pressure will feel the effects of fatigue build-up.

Many company incentive schemes today are based on performance, which is calculated in the main from standard times. As a general rule, there is no ceiling on performance for payment purposes, and thus by implication management are accepting high performance, and high bonus. In the early theories, performance should not rise too high, because fatigue build-up would prevent an operator working beyond a certain point. In practice, there are many ways round this theory. Thus the bonus proportion of earnings gets larger, and larger. Operators soon begin to feel that a 100 performance is the minimum to aim for, and often do not feel a full sense of satisfaction even at 100 performance. High performances are soon taken for granted, and standard times are *expected* to yield high bonus. The fact is that the 100 performance is a good average. This aspect was discussed fully at the end of Chapter Two.

Here the emphasis must be on the concept of relaxation allowance. In British Standard thinking, relaxation allowances are evaluated for an assumed performance level of 100. Any operator that believes he can both achieve very high performances and return home without being tired, is in principle quite wrong. Other means to enhance his pay should be found, not abuse of the incentive scheme, or even his own health. Fortunately, more and more companies are beginning to see the wisdom of having a ceiling on bonus earnings. In the longer term, control over levels of performance, based on consideration for the employees, must be the best answer.

Surely no one is against a high standard of living for all; the higher the better. Using the payment system helps to achieve this when first introduced, as it should; it is wrong to try to use the incentive scheme itself as a continuous process of improvement. It is quite illogical, and must inevitably fail. No matter how much can be gained after the initial planned impact, there must come a time when the payment system will fail to yield further benefit to the employee. In time it *will* cause disputes, when fair times are issued, but are not considered to be high enough to earn high performance, without excessive fatigue. Any attempt to do so will only add fatigue through worry and frustration to fatigue from excessive efforts. The company is right in principle to issue times that are sound, the employees are right in practice when they claim they are unable to earn the high performances that have been authorised in the past. The high performances are rarely a true reflection of the actual performance; they are merely out-of-date standards. Hence, for operators on new times to earn the same money without undue fatigue, they must consider mis-booking, leaving safety guards open, reducing quality, or even going on strike to have the times made more generous. They cannot beat the fatigue itself, so the time or the methods must change.

A standard time should be a *standard* like any other. A higher standard of living will only ultimately be achieved by improved productivity, sound planning, a sound payment system, and a fair and reasonable effort. As the amount of relaxation allowance is related to the job being done, and built into the standard time, anyone working at 100 performance should be taking approximately the right amount of rest.

Modern scientific measurement of work is used as a basis for issuing times for specified tasks, performed under specified conditions, and at a defined level of performance. It has already been explained that when using British Standard the defined level of performance is a 100 performance.

The fundamental basis of the 100 performance is that the operator should be able to work at 100 *rating* on average, while actually working. It is also recognised that the operator will need to take rest pauses from time to time in order that he can continue working at a 100 rating. It is indeed internationally recognised that the human being is not able to maintain a brisk pace of working for long periods without a pause. To overcome this problem, it is totally accepted that operators stop working for three basic reasons.

1   To recover from the fatigue of working at 100 rating.
2   To fulfil personal needs as required naturally.
3   To take relief from environmental pressures.

It is thus possible to establish two distinct ways of measuring the effort of working.

1   The rate of working of an operator, whilst actually working: RATING.
2   The average performance of an operator, or operators, over a long period such as a day, having taken the rest that the work demands: PERFORMANCE.

The problem of establishing a true performance base is twofold.

1   Measuring how long carefully specified jobs should take at a 100 rating over a short period. This is done, perhaps, by time study, making rating assessments for all observed elements. There are, of course, other work measurement techniques, and some have the rating factor built into the time.
2   Assessing the amount of relaxation allowance the work demands, within the attendance time, so that the qualified operator can average a 100 rating while working, should they choose to do so throughout the working period.

The Difficulties of Assessing Relaxation Allowance

The assessment of relaxation allowance is by no means a simple task, nor one that should be treated lightly. Clearly level of accuracy is relevant here, so that category A and B work should be considered more carefully than category C work.

Relaxation allowance may be applied either to each element, or to the job as a whole. Quite possibly, for category C work, one could apply it once to the total. After all the job is only temporary, and accepted as being fairly inaccurate! For category A and B type jobs, there are some companies where it is agreed to use one standard figure. This is where the work is very much the same throughout the department, and is unlikely to change. Generally, however, it is strongly recommended that each element be considered separately. To understand fatigue fully, you should read a book on ergonomics, and consider very closely the implications of *static and dynamic* effort. One can easily tend to assess relaxation allowance from the amount of effort one 'sees' from the 'movement' in the job. The strain is more likely to come from static effort than from dynamic effort. To understand what static effort is, the reader is asked to stand quite still for five minutes, with the hands held on top of the head. It is critical in this experiment that you attempt *to remain absolutely motionless*. This is not possible, but it is important to try. You will feel the effort. Then consider if there are any jobs under your control where the operator has to hold a set position in order to do the job. Examples are typists, operators at conveyor belts, and many highly repetitive jobs. The typist chair was designed specifically to overcome this type of problem. The fatigue does not take place in the moving parts of the body until well after the static parts have 'forced' the operator to take a rest.

Although there are no rules, it is generally accepted that somewhere between 8 and 10% would be the *minimum* figure for any industrial job. The largest allowance personally experienced is 100%. In this latter case, there was a costly furnace that needed to be kept working or the work of a whole team was held up, as well as causing quality problems. Evaluated relaxation allowance was nearing 70% for the job. Rather than allow a single operator to stop for such a long proportion of the day, it was agreed that two operators would be employed and would keep the furnace running at all times it was needed.

Balancing Work Patterns to Reduce Fatigue

In considering elements individually, it should be remembered that a series of strenuous elements are far more tiring when they run consecutively, and particularly so if the body has to hold a specific position. Hence, when interspersed with elements requiring quite different muscles to be used, relaxation allowance is much lighter. In practice the operator can take 'relaxation' while working to cover *some* of the fatigue. The effects of fatigue can be reduced by planning the method so that

155

contrasting types of element provide changes in the demand on the operator, both mentally and physically. Mental concentration can be relieved by a set of manual elements, and a monotonous job can be made less tedious by arranging that the operator has responsibility away from the main workpoint. If the job is badly designed, remember that the operator *will have to take rest*. It can be quite valuable to allow the operators to do their own inspection, calculate their own bonus, or similar ideas. Naturally, there may need to be additional spot checks.

This may appear to conflict with the principles of motion economy, and if it does the answer lies in compromise. It is slowly being understood that if the work pattern is too efficient it leads to a need for greater relaxation when not working. It may even be that absenteeism and strikes are in themselves a form of relaxation taken by the operators. Perhaps this concept is best left to the sociologists, but people interested in the design of work must be aware of their research. Other studies have shown that the faster fatigue build-up occurs so the time to recover increases even more rapidly. Hence, total efficiency is greater *if short rest pauses are taken as needed by the individual* than if a long work spell is attempted.

Clear examples are difficult to find, but consider an athlete running 100 metres. The duration of high effort is very short, but the duration of fatigue recovery is very long. If an employer were to employ someone as a runner to transmit important messages, would it be wiser to ask them to run at high speed, thus incurring high fatigue, then rest, then run, then rest, than to ask them to run at a more leisurely pace, taking rest pauses less frequently?

In making relaxation allowance, then, one is merely recognising that an average operator on bonus will simply not be able to maintain that steady pace for several hours on end without a pause for rest. He will either gradually slow down, as fatigue builds up, or as an alternative stop altogether. Even for the operator not on bonus, rest pauses are necessary, and can even be as high as someone on bonus. Due to static work, the operator that works at a slower pace can become equally tired as a fast worker. After all both may have to hold the same body position in order to complete the job. The arms may be moving at different speeds, but the static work, the cause of the greatest fatigue, is the same for both operators.

There is a ráte of working where the speed of dynamic movement begins to play an increasing part in fatigue. This probably occurs at around 110 performance, though not enough research has been done on this aspect of fatigue. When measuring people at work, the work study officer is looking for someone specially selected and trained to do the work. Such operators should be capable of working at 100 rating without too much dynamic effort. Slowing down would be easy, speeding up more difficult. Speeding up from 100 rating either means working with above average skill or building up fatigue rapidly, thus forcing longer rest periods.

Personal Needs Allowance

As a general rule, personal needs allowance is given as a flat percentage. Traditionally, women have always been given 1 or 2% more than men. With the recent introduction of sex equality legislation in Britain, a favourite question amongst the professionals is: 'are the ladies still given the extra %?'

For the moment, there is no answer to this question; that has been agreed. It is still left to each individual company to reach its own conclusion. There have been hints that in interpreting the law women will continue to have this slight advantage.

Factors in Fatigue Allowance

Fatigue allowance, however, must be related to the nature of the work, and the conditions in which it is performed. Fatigue allowance can be divided into three main categories.

1 Fatigue caused by the environment in which the work is performed, e.g. temperature, light.
2 Fatigue caused by the actual use of body muscles, e.g effort, posture.
3 Mental fatigue, e.g. worry, monotony.

The environmental causes of fatigue should not present any significant problems as it is possible in the main to measure these conditions scientifically.

Light – Lumens
Heat – Temperature
Noise – Decibels

A large amount of research has been completed into the effects of environment, and tables evaluated. An example of one of these special tables is given at the end of this chapter. The tables should be used in conjunction with a book on ergonomics. Advice is given in such books on the optimum conditions for a wide range of work types. It is at this point that the professional *should consider improving these conditions* as an alternative to making allowances. This assumes that this has not been done during method study, or is even covered by legislation. For example, the professional is advised by his institute that the manager should be advised in writing if lighting is poor, rather than just allow relaxation allowance to cover this. The object is to avoid clashes with the Health and Safety Acts. It is the responsibility of the manager either to improve the lighting, or to 'insist' on an allowance. The professional must not automatically give allowances.

Understanding Muscular Fatigue

The amount of fatigue caused by muscles and the natural fatigue recovery while actually working will cause the most problems. The first principle to accept is that this assessment must be made assuming that four conditions have already been met.

1   The operator is qualified.
2   The operator will be encouraged, even 'controlled', to work at an average performance of 100.
3   Personal needs allowance is adequately covered.
4   Environmental and mental allowances are adequately covered, and thus the work can be seen as being performed in economic or 'optimum' conditions.

It is the *nature* of muscle fatigue that must be most carefully considered. The following examples are suggested as a means of aiding evaluation in this matter. Beware, however, as there are no clear-cut rules. First consider lifting a chair with one hand. This is done in the first instance from one of the back legs, as shown in fig. 65. The initial muscle strain will be taken by the

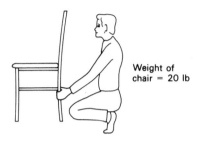

Weight of
chair = 20 lb

Fig. 65   Lifting a chair from the floor with one hand.

shoulders, arm, wrist and hand, as the weight of the chair is taken off the floor. Next, muscle strain is added to the operator's legs and back, as they straighten up. The original strain continues while standing. As the standing position is reached, the effort is very slightly reduced in the upper limbs and shoulder, and substantially reduced in the legs.

During the lift, the chair is trying to move in three different ways, as shown in fig. 66.

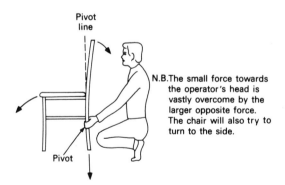

Pivot
line

N.B. The small force towards
the operator's head is
vastly overcome by the
larger opposite force.
The chair will also try to
turn to the side.

Pivot

Fig. 66   The arrows show the gravitational forces against which the operator must lift.

Turn the chair 180°, and although it is the same weight the strain on the muscles is different, due to the law of mechanics. See fig. 67.

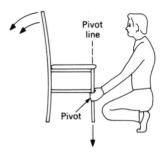

Fig. 67   Turning the chair round changes the gravitational forces on the chair, and the effort on the operator.

Finally, using the same chair, this time it is placed on a table. The lift is again quite different from the previous two lifts, as the work is done almost entirely with the hand, the wrist, the arm and the shoulder. The lift is illustrated in fig. 68.

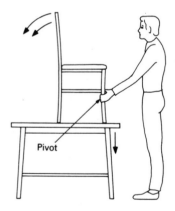

Fig. 68   Here there is not only a smaller lift to be made but the posture of the operator makes lifting easier.

In this chair-lifting example, it is the same chair that is being lifted in each case. It requires very little imagination on the part of the reader to realise that the fatigue build-up will be quite different in each case. Should there be any doubt, the exercise can be quickly reproduced in the home or office!

In the second exercise we shall consider an operator lifting a jig, full of metal pieces, into a bath of acid. On this occasion one is again considering the significance of weight and effort, but in this case even more factors are included.

The task is to lift a batch of metal strips to a bath for electro-etching. It has been agreed in this case that the maximum weight to be lifted is 50 lb for a man. The work is done in a 'wet section', and the floor is subsequently very slippery. To help overcome this problem, duck boards have been laid in front of the bath of acid. These not only keep the feet out of the water, but also reduce the height from floor to bench surface. Method improvement is clearly needed, but for the purpose of the exercise ignored, as indeed it was by this particular company!

Two elements are considered.

Element 1: Load jig with metal strips, one at a time. (This part is quite easy on the muscles, as only one piece is loaded at a time.)

Element 2: Lift full jig clear of bench, reach forward over tank, and then lower jig into acid bath. Secure ends of jig on hooks and release. (Because of the danger from acid splash, the jig needed to be lowered slowly into the acid.) The duckboard was inevitably wet and sticky. If one was to simulate this as an exercise, one discovers that it is necessary to rise onto one's toes and almost risk rupture. *Some* of the relaxation from fatigue in this element would most probably be taken immediately at the end of the element, and before proceeding to the next.

To illustrate this even more clearly the two elements are shown alongside one another in fig. 69. In the first element only one piece is being lifted at a time. In the second there is a weight factor and considerable potential danger.

161

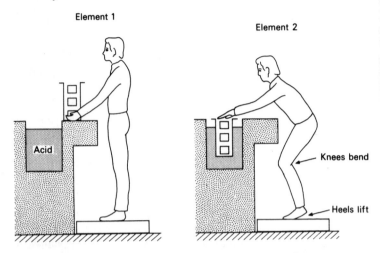

Fig. 69   Two quite different postural positions, plus the extra fatigue due to needing slow movements.

High Fatigue Allowance means Arduous Effort

It has been suggested on more than one occasion, and with some justification, that a very high fatigue allowance is an admission that the work is exceptionally arduous. It is a prime objective of trade unions to reduce such cases, where possible, by seeking improved working conditions. It is a prime objective of work study professionals to achieve the same end, by improving working methods. Therefore there should be no conflict of view or intention in this matter.

Fatigue, being compounded of so many mental and physical factors, is very difficult to measure. Methods of limited use have been devised for measuring some of the effects of fatigue in the laboratory. In the main, these could not be used in any other way than for research. Nevertheless, these laboratory experiments have produced valuable data, which tends to have been proven as reasonable. It is still difficult to transfer this data directly into the commercial application of standard times. It should be remembered that, if a time is quickly prepared, it will

162

probably soon become loose over-all, and even too little relaxation allowance will be accepted. In aiming for a more precise measurement and control of the work content, it becomes imperative that relaxation allowance is more carefully assessed.

In the research referred to above, studies for typical jobs were taken over a long period, sometimes spanning days. During these studies, it was possible to observe how rest was taken, as well as how much. One can still do this prior to issuing specific standard times, perhaps measuring contingencies, at the same time. The means to do this would be normal production study.

Relaxation Allowance Tables

The result of all the work that has been done is the development of relaxation allowance tables, for day to day use. This is now generally accepted as the most practical way, although it still leaves room for debate. In one nationalised industry, for example, it was suggested and accepted that the few tables available for general use did not fit the work of that industry. A set of tables was thus specially prepared and agreed with the trade union before they were used. As a matter of interest, in that same agreement over incentives, it was also agreed that there should be a ceiling of 100 performance for payment purposes, and to avoid excessive effort.

The tables are built up after separating the causes of fatigue into categories or factors. Precise definitions of these factors should be included. Each factor is given a range of percentage allowances, with guidance about which figure to select. In many cases, typical job examples are given to guide the analyst.

It is important here to distinguish between the estimation of the operator's effort by rating, and the assessment of the fatigue allowance demanded by the work. Rating compares the operator's 'performance' at that moment with the observer's concept of a *standard performance* of the job in question. In forming his concept of this 'performance' or rating, the observer will take into account the weight of the parts, the distances moved, and the precision and complexity of the movements required. He will visualise an incentive rate of working for the particular job. No extra allowance should be given for fatigue in the rating assessment.

A simple example is the one where the operator lifts a jig full of metal pieces into an acid bath. This is a very arduous task at that moment. First it should be remembered that the operator would have been specially selected and trained for this work. The circumstances of the job will encourage the operator to work at a specific speed. To attempt to do the job faster is quite dangerous; to do it more slowly would be backbreaking, and also dangerous. In other words there is really only one speed the operator can work at, and the element should thus be rated at 100. It is relaxation allowance that will take care of the fatigue, not the rating. On one occasion, the author worked for a company where some sacks of wheat had to be carried across a room. Each sack weighed 200 lb. There was no way in which you could be encouraged to speed up or slow down, once that weight was on your back!

In determining the fatigue allowance, the work study professional will consider all those factors which prevent the operator from continuing to work at a 100 rating. These same factors will literally prevent the operator from working much above 100, and allowances must be made accordingly.

One principle should always be first to reduce the factors causing fatigue, but, for any fatigue still inherent in the job: *allow time to recover from that fatigue.*

In his books, Frederick Taylor wrote of the advantages he found in introducing organised rest pauses. Today, of course, in most companies, the mid-morning and mid-afternoon rest pauses are widely accepted. It is generally conceded that if such rest pauses are not allowed officially other means of taking rest pauses will be devised, thus making supervision more difficult. Unofficial rest pauses are not considered fully effective anyway, as the operators will not fully relax if they know they are breaking the rules.

To illustrate the principle of relaxation allowance tables, an example has been made up consisting of four pages. The first page is fictional and should not be used to assess allowances. The next three pages simply demonstrate the application and analysis of the allowances made. First, the fictional table is shown in fig. 70.

	Factor	Detail	Example	Percentage
1	Effective Effort	Very Light Light Medium Heavy Very Heavy	(Using the example of lifting a jug into an acid bath) Lift weight into bath of acid	2 5 15 25 ⑤0
2	Posture	Seated Standing Leaning Bending	Lean forward on toes	0 2 ⑤ 10
3	Motions of arms	Natural Non-R Natural Rep Unnatural	Hold arms out straight	⓪ 5 8
4	Eyestrain	See book on Ergonomics	Well lighted section	⓪ 4 8 12
5	Personal Needs	Male Female	Males only on this work	③ 5
6	Temperature	See book on Ergonomics	Enclosed room Temp 70	0 ② 6 10
7	Atmospheric	See book on Ergonomics	Light acid fumes	0 5 ⑫ 20
8	Other factors	Routine Monotony Worry Anything!	Quite an interesting job in total	⓪ 3 5 ?

Fig. 70   Fictional relaxation allowance table using 'Lift jug to acid bath' as a typical job.

The next two pages, shown in figs. 71 and 72, have been devised for use in conjunction with the table. The principle here is that the allowance is decided upon after discussion by two people. Details about the element are given in determining the selected percentage. A third column is given, in case a record is felt advisable, about the reasons or doubts for the selected percentage. Finally, the figures are checked by the Head of Department or section leader to establish consistency and skill of application.

Element No. ONE		Ref. No. E.E./27/3	
Description Pick up one metal piece and locate on jig. Ensure no two pieces touch.			
Factor	**Detail**	**Selected**	**Comments**
1 Effective Effort	Very light work. Pick up one piece, about 1 lb at a time	2 %	Can change hands
2 Posture	Normal standing position	2 %	Can balance from one foot to another
3 Motion of the arms	Natural, and can vary method slightly	0 %	—
4 Eyestrain	Well lighted section 60 lumens	0 %	Natural occasional focus
5 Personal Needs	Males only on this job	3 %	—
6 Temperature	Temperature a little warm 70°	2 %	Not much fresh air
7 Atmospheric	Close to acid fumes but they are very slight here	5 %	Discuss extraction with Manager? S.O
8 Other Factors	Fairly interesting job in total, and can talk to colleagues	0 %	—
Total R.A.		14 %	Date 27/2/80
Comments Difficult to assess effects of acid. Discuss with Manager and Safety Officer		Prepared by R.T.G. M.R.J. Authorised by Tony A. Jay	

Fig. 71 Calculation of relaxation allowance for a fairly straightforward job (for illustration purposes only).

Element No. __TWO_____		Ref. No. __E.E./27/3___	
Description __Lift jig (50 lb) into acid bath._____			

Factor	Detail	Selected	Comments
1 Effective Effort	Lift 50 lb into acid bath. Lean on to toes Very strenuous	50%	This job is really quite dangerous and should be improved
2 Posture	Standing, but leaning forward on toes with knees bent	5%	Extra care needed to ensure balance
3 Motion of the arms	Basically little movement with arms	0%	—
4 Eyestrain	Well lighted section 60 lm²<15	0%	Can look round on elements one and three
5 Personal Needs	Males only on this job	3%	—
6 Temperature	Temperature a little warm 70°	2%	Not much fresh air
7 Atmospheric	Light acid fumes immediately over bath	12%	Department checked and fumes are largely dissipated
8 Other Factors	Fairly interesting job, and can talk to colleagues	0%	—
Total R.A.		72%	Date 27/2/80

Comments Operator takes some R.A. immediately after completing this element and before starting the next one	Prepared by ___R.T.G.___ ___M.R.J.___ Authorised by Tony A. Jay

Fig. 72 Calculations of relaxation allowance for a very arduous element (for illustration purposes only).

On the fourth page, shown in fig. 73, one simply shows how the allowance can, in some instances, be placed directly onto the sheet where the standard times are calculated. This is an alternative approach to the previous example. This can sometimes be used in category C work.

El. Ref.	Element Description	Total BMs	No. of Occs.	BMs per Occ.	Freq./piece	BMs per piece	1	2	3	4	5	6	7	8	Total	Work Content Basic	U.T.A.	Work Content Basic
	Unit of output: One metal piece	**From Summary Sheet**					**Relaxation Allowance**											
1	Load metal piece to jig	24.000	480	0.050	1/1	0.050	2	2	0	0	3	2	5	0	14			0.057
2	Load full jig to acid bath	2.400	12	0.200	1/40	0.005	50	5	0	0	3	2	12	0	72			0.009
3	Switch on tank power																	
4	Unload completed jig																	
5	Unload pieces from jig		Example for R.A.													N.B.		
6	Switch off tank power		purposes only.													The average		
7	Obtain new box of pieces															relaxation		
																allowance		
																for these two		
																elements is only		
																20%		

Dept. Electro-Etching	Sect. Acid Bath	Set up 27/3	Date 27/2/80	Ref. EE/27/3 Sh. 1 of 1

Fig. 73 Allocation of relaxation allowance to BMs.

The skill with which relaxation allowances are applied will depend very much on the company policy on work measurement. This will consider the many implications, the acceptance or rejection of levels of accuracy, before the final approach is chosen.

The largest danger involved in the whole field of work measurement, which can lead to all sorts of unnecessary costs, is lack of knowledge. On the one hand, managers and accountants may urge for the speedy preparation of data, for its obvious use benefits. Yet, at the same time, they may quite happily employ inexperienced practitioners. By unwittingly putting inexperienced practitioners under pressure, through unrealistic target dates for completion, the data provided must be suspect. If such suspect data was rarely seen, this statement need not be made, but poor data is so widespread and virtually uncontrolled in many cases so as to be almost frightening. It is inevitable that this lack of wisdom and control will lead to wages protection, wages drift and wages disputes. No one in the long run gains; neither the company nor the employees.

When a company, with full knowledge and careful analysis, decides that relatively junior staff, producing data in a hurry, is in the best interests of the company and its employees, so be it. Such a company should also advise its work study practitioners that it is the *policy* to work in this way. Indeed, the unions should be advised also. In this way, and under a specified policy, there should be no complications.

Assuming that policy demands that work measurement should be very professionally prepared, that levels are accepted, and that professionals of high skill are employed, then relaxation allowances should also be very thoroughly detailed. In the definition for time study, one finds that the requirements of work measurement are not only that the work be clearly specified, but also the *conditions*.

It is not the intention of this book to urge for higher standards as a blind principle. The concepts make sound business and economic sense. There is a third choice that directors can make, and often do. This is not to have work measurement at all. The three choices are as follows.

169

1   A simple work measurement based system, *essentially* protected by having a ceiling on the bonus proportion.
2   A professional work measurement based system, *preferably* protected by having a ceiling on the bonus proportion.
3   Consider very seriously not having work measurement at all, if it is not to be done well.

N.B. Too many companies today have choice 1 but *think* they have choice 2.

The Taking of Rest Pauses

This chapter could not be complete without some reference to the taking of rest pauses. Having concluded that rest pauses are not only necessary but should also be included in the standard times, the operators must then, of course, take those rest pauses.

There are clearly quite a number of ways in which this can be done. For obvious reasons, this must be within the area of responsibility of the manager. It is not normally considered to be part of the work study function to decide how and when relaxation allowance should be taken. The work study responsibility stops at advising on the minimisation of fatigue causes, plus ensuring that provision is made in the time. Sometimes, where relief operators are used to ensure that expensive or key equipment can continue to function, work study can act in an advisory role.

Some of the ways of taking rest pauses are listed below.

1   Official tea breaks.
2   Just stopping when the operator needs to rest the muscles.
3   Provision of relief operators.
4   Working at a slower pace.
5   Making minor but approved variations in method. This should not reduce quality or safety levels.
6   Job rotation.

Clearly, the best long-term view to take is to design the work so that fatigue and fatigue causes are kept at a minimum. The steps to achieve this may include simple method study, improving the environment, or even job enrichment.

Job enrichment, or job enlargement, is not considered to be part of the subject of this book, though there is a link. The reader is thus encouraged to study this as a separate subject.

Chapter Eleven

Other Allowances

When building up standard times, there are a number of factors other than normal elements, contingencies, and relaxation allowance. In some cases concerning times they are not necessary; in others they are quite fundamental to the work inherent in the job. This area of study is known quite often as 'other allowances'. In total there are nine, ten or eleven; the major ones are dealt with briefly here. Enough information is provided in this chapter for the *appreciation* of the allowance covered. It is left to the practitioner, dealing with specific items, to deal thoroughly with the analysis of fair and logical allowances. Where the need for an allowance arises, the professional should be able to make provision in the issued times. The allowances dealt with, very briefly, in this chapter are as follows.

1 Contingencies – an extension to the coverage already made.
2 Unoccupied time allowances.
3 Attention time.
4 Interference time.
5 Reject allowances.

Allowances not included in Standard Times

In addition to allowances that are included as part of the standard time there is also a series of allowances which can be given in addition to the standard times, *but which are normally issued quite separately*. These may include the following.

1 Daily allowances.
2 Batch allowances or setting-up allowances.
3 Material or machine allowances.

4   Run in and run out allowances.
5   Training allowances.
6   Policy allowances or bonus increments.

These two lists are not intended to be exhaustive, but demonstrate some of the complications of using measured work standards, and help in the construction of other relevant allowances.

Allowances can begin to take up a large proportion of a working day. Once given they can be difficult to reduce or withdraw, so great care and experience is needed in their preparation.

The Contingency Allowance

The contingency allowance is divided into two parts, though it is debatable if this is really necessary. There are work contingency allowances and delay contingency allowances. The major principle is to decide whether work or delay studied during a time study should be allowed as a contingency, or extracted as a foreign element or ineffective time. Assuming it is to be allowed, it becomes necessary to prepare a contingency set-up sheet, related to the set-up sheet for occasional and repetitive elements. The percentage contingency allowance for each study is calculated, and finally a full summary is made. The contingency allowance shown in these calculations is then added to the over-all cycle time of the job, *after* relaxation allowance has been included. In this way there is no need to put relaxation allowance directly onto contingencies. In fact the contingency allowance receives the average relaxation allowance that has been added to the main elements.

Total BMs   =   2.500 ⎱
Add 5% contingency allowance   =   0.125 ⎰ 2.625
Total BMs plus relaxation allowance =   2.800 ⎱
Add 5% contingency allowance   =   0.140 ⎰ 2.940

It should be accepted that some contingency type 'elements' will not have been seen at all. These are compensated for, because those that are seen are given a higher frequency than would normally occur.

Unoccupied Time Allowance

Unoccupied time occurs when an operator is waiting for a machine element or process time to finish before he can continue working. It is customary for such time to be allocated at a 100 rating. The operator is only said to be unoccupied when he is not recovering from fatigue, or actually working, but is staying at his post, because the machine or process may need his attention. It is quite possible, during the governing element, or process, that the operator may be engaged in inside work, taking some relaxation allowance, or even giving essential attention to the machine. An illustration is given in fig. 74 to

Load (manual)	Machine time (Governing element)				Unload (manual)	Part R.A.
	Inside work	Part R.A.	Attention time	Unoccupied time		

Fig. 74   A standard time build-up, and how it should be structured.

show how several allowances occur within the same standard time. The taking of relaxation allowance should be discussed and agreed. As a general rule, where machine cycles are very short, and one can switch on and off at will, relaxation should be taken outside the machine operation times. In other words, the operator just switches off and takes authorised rest without having to worry about the machine. When the machine cycle, however, is very long, and very costly to stop, relaxation can often be taken inside the machine governing element while it is still working. This may be done by just relaxing, or may involve relief operators. In either event *the taking of relaxation* must be agreed by all concerned.

Attention Time

During machine running times, it is often necessary for the machine operator to make minor adjustments, or simply 'keep a close eye' on the satisfactory running of the machine. This is work and must be recognised as such. It cannot be relaxation allowance, nor unoccupied time allowance. The operator would be undertaking management specified attention to the machine. An allowance must be given. The measurement of attention time can be very difficult, and should be dealt with only by experienced professionals.

Interference Allowance

A further allowance closely related to the above two examples is known as interference allowance. This occurs when an operator is operating more than one machine. Interference is said to occur when the operator is busily engaged on one machine, and another automatically stops. As the operator cannot work on two machines at a time, there is an interference in production. The more machines that an operator is asked to operate, the greater the build-up in interference time. Clearly, the operator must be given times to cover this loss of production. Perhaps the most common example of this case is in the loom department of a textile mill. With automatic loom operations, it is quite common for weavers to operate quite a number of machines. In the case of looms, with a random pattern of machine stoppages, statistical means have to be found to determine the interference allowance to be given. Activity sampling or tables such as Ashcroft tables may be used. Even so, time study is used in many cases to establish the basic elemental times, and can be used in check or production studies.

When the operator operates several machines, and the pattern of times is more precise, such as in engineering production, the interference allowance can be calculated by preparing a multiple activity chart. The times for this chart may well have been prepared from basic time studies.

Reject Allowance

The last example of allowance to be given, for those aspects of the job that are built into the standard times, is the reject allowance. This allowance is usually calculated in the form of a frequency. Assume that in producing work some rejects are unavoidable, and thus accepted by management. The method of calculation that allows for these rejects is first to prepare the standard time and then to multiply it by a *reject frequency*. An example is given below. In the example, the standard time for preparing work, or loading a machine, is 3.000 SMs per box. The normal reject levels acceptable to management are that 5 are lost in every 100. The issued standard time is calculated thus:

$$\frac{3.000 \text{ SMs} \times 100}{95} = \frac{3.158}{\text{or } 3.16 \text{ SMs/box}}$$

The operator is asked to record only those boxes that are passed as satisfactory. No time is allowed separately for the rejects.

Complex Nature of Allowances

As the application of all these allowances, where appropriate, can become quite complicated, the final analysis must be made by experienced staff, or professionals. To attempt to explain all the complexities here is considered too difficult.

To emphasise both the complexity and the significance, it may be useful to quote one case history. In a textile concern, which had over 300 automatic looms, considerable concern was expressed by the employees that the standard times were causing problems. During an investigation lasting several months, and being 'taunted' by a possible series of strikes, industrial relations suffered quite seriously. Both sides were being very reasonable, in that they *both believed that they were right*. The problem, however, of interference and other allowances was never fully understood by either the company or the employees. All that was necessary to resolve the difference of opinion was a greater understanding of how the standard times were based, and best applied. Both employer and employee lost.

Daily and Batch Allowances

Allowances that are not included in the standard time, as a general rule, are much easier to establish and handle.

Daily allowances and batch allowances are simply given in this way because of their frequency of occurrence. When something occurs only once per day, or once per batch, it is more logical to issue a separate standard time for that work than to attempt to build it into the standard time for a job. Of course, one can decide to build it into the values, but it is probably best to separate such work.

Machine or Material Allowances

A machine or material allowance, or even some other types, is added to the standard time, where appropriate, on a temporary basis. If, for example, a machine has to be run at below the normal speed, for technical reasons, one can measure for and calculate a special allowance to cover the delays. As soon as work returns to normal, the allowance is withdrawn. The same applies to materials, when due to quality or other reasons the job is performed more slowly. It is not the fault of the operator, and to avoid loss of earnings this extra time is given. A simple example may be when an issued standard time is 2.0 SMs per piece. A request is made for a machine allowance. A temporary time at category C level can be quickly prepared. Assume this temporary time is calculated at 2.5 minutes. Then the original standard time is used, but a machine allowance of
2.5 minus 2.0 = 0.5 minutes per piece is given.
For subsequent allowances a new study should be taken.

Run In and Run Out Allowances

Occasionally, when operating certain jobs, such as loading a baking furnace, there is a period of time at the beginning and again at the end of a cycle, when work is being, say, loaded but not unloaded. At a later part of the cycle, work will be unloaded, but no more is being loaded. To cover this time, it is quite common to calculate a run in and run out allowance. The multiple activity chart is quite a useful way of calculating and explaining the allowance to management and employees.

Training Allowances

Training allowances are given by some companies as an encouragement to employees. Again full of complexities. Essentially, they should be prepared with great care, using logic as the base, and agreed between management and employees. The amount of time spent on their preparation depends on the company. One can discuss and agree arbitrary figures, or even move into the study of learning curves, and systematic training. Whichever route is chosen, someone with experience should be consulted or they may prove to be cumbersome.

Policy Allowances or Bonus Increments

The final allowance to be mentioned here is the policy allowance or bonus increment. They should never need to be used where there is a sound policy on work measurement and a carefully controlled incentive scheme. However, once the scheme begins to fall apart because it is badly designed, these special allowances have been designed to protect the professional work measurer. The person completing work measurement should be *asked to prepare sound times as far as practical*. If they prove to be out of line with existing loose standards, then management can carry the responsibility of inconsistency of times by giving special allowances, aimed at retaining a consistent pattern of earnings. This is a negative approach, no doubt, but when it is too late what else can be done?

When such an allowance is added to the standard time, it is issued as an allowed time and *not* a standard time.

Chapter Twelve

Finalising and Issuing Standard Times

In the chapter on industrial relations, a strong emphasis was placed on good communications. A high level of co-operation on the preparation and issue of standard times can hardly be expected if too little time is spent on discussion. After all, the times issued are to affect the rate at which an employee works, the amount of money earned each week, the amount of rest taken, and even the transfer of operators to other sections, yet there are two distinct ways in which times are normally distributed. These are often called the traditional and modern methods. Fig. 75 compares the two systems.

The author believes that *in principle* the traditional method is obsolete. There are, of course, many companies that still use this approach, and it is quite possible that the calculation of standard times is very precise and accurate. It is also possible that the number of studies taken and the professional quality is very high. Yet it is also possible that all is not well. Providing the system does work, perhaps it is well to continue with the tradition. It could be said that a deeper understanding and responsibility by management is not really needed.

In other cases, where the approach is the modern and more logical system, management will know more exactly how standard times are structured. They are, after all, making a direct contribution to the development and maintenance of those times.

So logical and precise is the build-up of standards that an understanding management will quickly grasp the analysis. In many cases, they will be responsible *for demanding improvements* in the system. There is no substitute, in any theory, that

Time Study

Traditional	Modern (Still rare)
Work Study Officer sometimes does Method Study and then studies the work. Eventually Standard Times are calculated. *No* information is divulged until actually finalised, and then first to the Manager Information tends to be restricted to the Standard Times themselves plus a brief Work Specification	Work Study Officer sometimes does Method Study. To commence the Work Measurement programme, the first stage is to agree with the manager that the method actually observed and to be studied by the Work Study Officer is the one approved by the Manager. (Manager asked to sign Ele. Description)
	Manager and Foreman receive copy of Element Description, and any queries during studies over method, or qualification of the operator can be referred to the Manager
	As studies continue, details from the Set-up Sheets, such as variances in time, frequencies etc. are discussed with the Manager and Foreman. Any queries are dealt with as they arise
	When it is agreed that sufficient studies have been taken the Standard Times can be calculated. Any allowances included can be discussed with Manager
	Eventually the Standard Times are completed, and the Manager is issued with not only the Standard Times, but also Work Specification Set-up Sheets and Calculation Sheets. Before issuing the Standard Times then, the Manager and his Foreman are not only familiar with all aspects, but have all the necessary data right from Element Description to completed times. All he does not have are the studies and general work in support, which is retained on file, yet available, by Management Services (Work Study)
A meeting is arranged to discuss Standard Times with employees and their representatives. This is usually on Friday afternoon, ready for a Monday morning start	Common to both Traditional and Modern
Discussion led by Manager, but passing many questions on the Standard Times to the Work Study Officer or Section Leader	Discussion led by Manager, who will answer many of the questions, but may refer any detailed ones to the Work Study Officer who did the Work Measurement, or led the team that made the actual studies

Fig. 75   Presentation of information to management, the labour force and their representatives, and its subsequent maintenance (assuming that the information consists of standard times for a new incentive application).

180

Traditional	Modern
Eventually in principle it will be agreed to TRY the Standard Times. It is emphasised that the employees have a RIGHT to checks, and that any errors will be put right	Common to both Traditional and Modern
During the Trial Period all queries will be directed to the Manager who normally passes them directly to the Work Study Department The Work Study Officer comes along and should first check the Method, conditions and equipment. He would refer any discrepancies back to the Manager for action e.g. the operator may not be using the correct method When everything is satisfactory, the Work Study Officer normally takes a detailed Check Study, and reports back, either with a changed time, or more frequently that he can find nothing wrong	During the Trial Period all queries will be directed to the Manager who will ask his Foreman to have a look at the situation. Method, conditions, equipment, frequencies, can all be looked at within the Department Assuming all appears to be fine, the Manager will ask The Work Study Department to come and do a thorough study. The operator should be qualified, as confirmed by the Foreman, and all equipment and facilities in order In many cases it is first advisable to complete a Production Study, perhaps using Systematic Sampling to determine why a section is not earning bonus, rather than starting with detailed Check Studies of the elements themselves
Following the survey, usually the Standard Times will be seen to be accepted. Either they will have been modified to the approval of the operators, or they will accept the original times We thus move to the period of time known as MAINTENANCE	Common to both Traditional and Modern
The Manager has not a great deal of information on precisely what the Standard Times are based upon, and is thus not equipped to recognise when minor changes take place. One could argue that he should know, but in many cases he *does not even know which method was actually studied*. How can he be expected then to know when changes have occurred and to what extent? Traditionally, then, when changes occur, the Work Study Department are not notified, and 'Wages Drift' begins: Who is responsible? NOBODY KNOWS	Manager has a specific responsibility to ensure that both Methods and Standard Times are carefully maintained. He also has the complete detail of method, indeed has signed his personal approval of that method. Consequently if that method, or the equipment or conditions change, he should know about it. He should also know that the time the job will take to complete has also probably changed. The Manager automatically calls in the Work Study Department. After all he is responsible, and that is the way it should be. The Work Study Department study will make any necessary adjustments
Industrial Relations not enhanced by this approach	Industrial Relations under the modern approach tend to be better than Traditional

181

will teach better than responsibility. Hence, the best way to understand times, and the implications, is for management to become involved with them, and responsible for the outcome.

It has been decided, therefore, not to attempt a comprehensive explanation of the final analysis, but to provide one simple and very basic illustration. Fig. 76 has been calculated directly from fig. 43. More complex examples including such allowances as interference and attention time should be learned by discussion of specific cases.

Clearly, in saying this, it can be assumed that discussion will take place anyway with the modern method. With the more traditional approach, the manager who wishes to know more must ask for this information to be made available. It will not in this situation be automatically provided.

Within any *company policy on work measurement*, there should be a statement concerning the approach adopted. Once this has been done, both management and work study will clearly understand their role and responsibility, in this important aspect of business. If it is not stated in company policy, one can almost safely assume that the traditional method will naturally occur. For any company that is suffering disputes, or is conscious that standard times are out of hand, or beginning to slide, just check on the company policy. If there is no policy on this aspect, it is the probable reason for the disintegration. If there is a policy on this aspect, stating the modern approach, then the managers are not meeting their stated responsibilities.

Demanding professional standards at the highest levels will pay financially over and over again. Accept low professional standards, if you must, but do not blame the professionals employed.

El. Ref.	Element Description	Total B.M.'s	No. of Occs.	BMs per Occ.	Freq./As-sembly	BMs per assembly	1	2	3	4	5	6	7	8	Total	Total SMs	U.T.A.	Issued SMs
1	Take and check two bolts	25·105	86	0·292	1/2	0·146	2	0	0	0	5	0	0	3	10			0·161
2	Put nut onto bolt	28·017	172	0·163	1/1	0·163	2	0	0	0	5	0	0	3	10			0·179
3	Bolts from tray	3·364	11	0·306	11/172	0·020	2	0	0	0	5	0	0	3	10			0·022
4	Nuts from tray	3·707	8	0·463	8/172	0·022	2	0	0	0	5	0	0	3	10			0·024
																	0·386
	Allow 5% for contingencies																0·405

Unit of output: Assemble Nut and Bolt

Standard Time for one assembly = 0·41

Dept.	Sect.	Set up for	Date	
Assembly	Nut and Bolt	assemble Nut and Bolt	Dec 14th 1979	Ref. N& 87 Sh. 1 of 1

Fig. 76 Simple illustration of calculation of a standard time.

Chapter Thirteen

The Uses of Work Measurement

There are six fundamental uses to which work measurement data is normally put. Many more are often quoted, yet one usually finds that they are merely variations on the basic six.

Standard Times and Prices

The first one to be discussed is the application in pricing, or estimating. The basis of any price has four different components.

1 Direct labour cost.
2 Direct material cost.
3 Overheads.
4 Profit margins.

At first glance, one could be forgiven for assuming that the data provided by work study is only critical in direct labour. In fact, it is connected very strongly to all areas, *except the direct material cost*. It is clear almost without explanation that times feature in labour cost analysis. All that needs to be emphasised here is that it is very easy to issue times that will quickly become obsolete, if they are not carefully prepared. Hence it can quickly happen that *actual* times to perform a task are quite different to the prices base.

Overheads are very much concerned with space and machine costs, or levels of output from machines. Transport costs, stores and many other items may be included in 'overheads'. For simplicity, an overhead is said to be a cost that cannot be allocated directly to a product. Even so, the efficiency with which the overheads are employed can cause the overhead proportion to vary. For example, the output from a machine may be largely governed by standard times. If the standard times on those machines are wrong, then the overhead allocation will also be wrong. If space and machines allocated to production are used badly, thus placing a limit, an unnecessary limit, on output or activity, the overheads have to be spread over a lower level of activity. Hence the greater the output from those machines and space, the smaller the overhead cost per unit.

Additionally, if the labour cost and the overhead cost are wrong, then the added profit margin and the price are wrong. This can mean that some prices are relatively high and the products less competitive. In others, the price is too low, and the product does not contribute enough to profit. It can be too easy for accountants just to accept times from work study, and *they have a responsibility to demand* that the data they use is solid and reliable. There need be no conflict between one profession and another, as all that is being suggested is that both are equally professional as specified in company policy. To employ two departments, one working at a high professional standard, and the other working at less than professional standard, may seem bad enough; but when the data of the professional department is heavily dependent for its *true* accuracy on the less professional department, *the value of both are diminished*. If there is any doubt about the implications expressed here, the accountant should be asked to give this concept the benefit of the doubt, and question quite deeply the implications for the company *if standard times are unreliable*.

Standard Times and Cost Control

The control of cost is also very much the field of the cost and management accountant. When developing the master budget, there is a number of budgets that are linked with the standard times. The sales budget may be limited by production capacity. Production capacity may eventually be limited by standard levels of output. The number of machines purchased and allowed for in the capital expenditure budget may well be dependent upon the standard levels of output of those machines. The biggest single saving on capital, due to revised standard times, and introduced by the author, was over £500,000, in the early 1970s. This followed a 'battle' between the author and the senior executives of his company. The author was losing the argument quite comfortably, until the production department concerned went on strike over the standard times. Until that action, the senior executives had decided that the advice offered was wrong. To avoid the strike, they took, very reluctantly, the advice of the author, and saved to their amazement £500,000 capital, and £60,000 per annum. Another budget, dependent to a large degree on standard times, will be the personnel budget. If times are wrong, the company will become 'overmanned'.

In reality, the skill with which standard times are prepared and issued can transform a company at best, and help it on the road to bankruptcy at worst.

Standard times are also basic to both standard costing and labour control systems.

The success of standard costing can often be considerably enhanced by good labour control. Yet even labour control can be based in such a way that it is not fully effective. Labour control should be developed with great skill to fit the section being controlled. Just to have a simple company-wide scheme may hide many possible savings. In one example, at an electricity board, cable laying was controlled by simple performance, waiting time, and other indices. By adding an analysis of the proportion of trench dug by hand and that dug by mechanical digger, and comparing that analysis to agreed targets, the cost of laying cable was almost halved. In fact, the manager had earlier been pleased by the high performances of his teams. A closer examination of figures booked, *before* authorising payment, caused the output to rise by 60% and the performances to fall from 110 to 100.

Standard Times and Planning

Times used for planning are again very much self-evident. It is not considered necessary to explain to the reader how this may be done. Any planning department can demonstrate the role

186

played by times in planning. The reason that times are best issued on a sound base, and subsequently controlled, is so that plans made, indeed, even promises to customers of delivery dates, are kept as planned. If the times issued, however, are allowed to become obsolete, and production levels allowed to rise above those predicted by the times, it does cause problems. Another major problem is when, to protect jobs and earnings, as they see it, the operators limit output to levels that they *judge* to be to their advantage. In many companies, the unions see the benefits of increasing output to a maximum, mainly because they have sound agreements which help to share the benefits of improved productivity. In other companies, where benefits are not shared quite so openly, there is less desire on the part of the employees to increase output. Nevertheless, change is inevitable. It does not make sense to go on planning on the same old times, year after year, if the production methods and levels of output are changing. The times should, therefore, accurately *reflect* the probable levels of output and cost. Even more, the times should *predetermine* those levels of output. As subsequent changes are valuable, then the times should be changed as a deliberate act of policy.

Standard Times and Training

When using work measurement as an aid to training, the concept of accuracy levels is once again a prime factor. Obviously, jobs that are expected to be made in low quantities may fall into category C type work. Times issued will be temporary, and so will the methods of operation. Training is of less importance, and so is element description for reasons of maintenance.

On jobs where the quantities are larger in number, there is more scope for establishing sound methods, and thus operators need training. As some operators leave the company, and the job and the method continues, newcomers need training to the authorised method. It is here that the work measurement procedures can be invaluable. Not only is there an accurate description of how the job is expected to be performed, but the description is broken into elements for which specific times are issued. From this base one can more quickly identify operator achievement, or weak points. In some cases, it is quite possible to develop a systematic training sequence.

As both quality and safety factors are built into the specified method, then achieving those factors plus target outputs are part of the training programme.

If successful training and monitoring of progress is to be achieved, then an adequate specification of the job method is vital. Where a sound work measurement policy already exists, the basis of training is built automatically into the measurement programme, and approved and controlled by the departmental manager.

Work Measurement and Evaluation

The purpose of evaluation in many respects is to support various calculations and arguments, prior to reaching a decision. There may be many areas of management where decisions are needed, and in which work measurement is not relevant. Yet knowledge of time can often be the basis of cost, and cost the basis of decision.

Frequently, the work measurement used is in the form of completed standard times. Present situations are often established on the basis of existing standards. Yet in so many cases, management wish to compare the present with the possible future, or even several future alternatives. The choice of technique may be activity sampling, P.M.T.S., time study, analytical estimating or synthetic data. It is quite common to use more than one technique in an investigation, but a useful example may be a time study on rolling mill operated by two men. Once studies have been completed, it may be possible to construct both a flow diagram and a multiple activity chart from the basic information. The very act of standing and observing the operators with a stopwatch enables the mind to begin the mental development of the new method. Once the evaluations have been made, to produce the improved method, the times are used to calculate the probable benefits of introducing the proposals.

Standard Times and Incentives

The final and possibly the most important use of standard times, and work measurement in general, is in the application of incentive bonus schemes. It is probably fair to say that this particular use has been partly covered throughout this book. The implications for the employees and managers in using standard times as the basis of payment must never be underestimated. The foolishness of not maintaining times to reflect existing methods is legend. On the other hand, so varied are the possible types of incentive scheme that they could not be reasonably covered here.

It should be sufficient to warn the reader that inconsistent times and badly structured incentive schemes will automatically and inevitably lead to grievances, disputes, high costs and poor industrial relations. Even the most thoroughly prepared and maintained schemes can cause problems, but at least they are minimal, and can be contained, or modified, without too many difficulties.

History has shown, in general, that poorly based work measurement systems do not necessarily lead to high wages, or a contented labour force. Rather the reverse is more in evidence. High wages and good industrial relations tend to go hand in glove with sound work measurement. Trade union representatives should not lightly seek inconsistencies in times or performance levels. It may seem at the time to be a minor 'victory', but in the longer term it simply will not work.

Chapter Fourteen

Planning for Change

In this final chapter, the implications that have been outlined in the book will be assessed. The subject of time study has naturally been covered in other books, but is usually limited to one chapter. It is thus not widely and deeply understood.

The concepts outlined can be of interest and value to work study professionals, managers, accountants, trade unionists, indeed many people. There are many many companies also to whom the subject of time study may be of interest. Any company that uses or is considering using work measurement can use the book to meet different needs. These companies are divided for simplicity into four categories.

1   Companies that use, or may use, work measurement but not normally time study.
2   Companies that have not yet commenced to introduce work study, or time study, into their systems, but may benefit by doing so.
3   Companies that have already introduced work study and time study, and where everything is well controlled.
4   Companies that have had work study and time study for a long time, but feel that things are beginning to slip, or may already have 'lost control'.

In the first group, the book may be of little value. Quite possibly, however, the principles could be useful in basic training. In addition to that, it is never known whether there is a potential time study project, if the principles are not fully understood.

The second group will be quite a significant one. Every year, several new companies will introduce work study for the first time. Clearly, in this case, the question of policy on work measurement, and selection of staff, is going to be a priority decision. The work study manager, appointed to a company where deep consideration has been given to the implications, is a very lucky manager indeed.

In the third group are those many companies who already use work study and time study, and where everything works well. Almost certainly there will be a carefully designed incentive bonus scheme, and an understanding management. Even so, the book will still prove useful as a basic training aid, and may even precipitate a number of modifications to the established system.

It is the last group that is not only the most serious but quite possibly the largest group. Here one will be dealing with precedent, tradition, even protectionism. By being 'out of control' it is meant that the standard times used by the company do not truly reflect the methods being used. As the vast bulk of these times will be loose, they will result in the bonus increment of pay being out of the normal proportion to basic wage. Also, as they will not be consistently loose, they will be the cause of quite a lot of discontent. It is inevitable in such cases that the employees, and the unions, will wish to ensure that the bonus proportion is retained. If management tried to correct the standard times, the unions would see this change as a direct attack on their wages, and therefore their standard of living.

Method study, which results in 'right' standard times to replace 'loose' ones, is thus naturally resisted. Departmental managers, often unwittingly, give support to this resistance. They often see successful method study as a reflection on their ability to manage. There are circumstances in which the union is right about earnings potential. The manager is often right about the reflection of his ability. In these combined circumstances, method study becomes virtually obsolete. It requires a change of circumstances to change this very inhibiting attitude. Only senior management can bring this about.

In the meantime, the remaining major benefit of work study is the provision of standard times, even though they are of doubtful accuracy. To protect earnings levels, it is clear that standard times must be as generous as existing ones. As the existing ones are already inconsistent in the bonus possibility they offer, how can one judge the 'reasonable looseness' of the new ones? Some companies even employ a person to negotiate from standard times to issued times. The union representatives will clearly want the times as loose as possible at the point of issue. Professional work measurement is protected by *management* adding a policy allowance; or bonus increment, to the standard times. Within months of issue, they will have become even more generous. The earlier issued times will have method changes and *acquired skill*, as the basis of looseness. The new ones will have the policy allowance as the means of making them equally loose, but will still have scope for acquiring skill. The new times, therefore, may soon be more generous than the old. Where does one stop? On the surface, management and unions will be arguing about times. The point really in contention, however, is wages rather than times.

The range of inconsistency grows even wider, and no one quite knows what a standard time is any more. Instead of leading to good industrial relations, these inconsistencies almost invariably lead to discussions, disillusionment, and bitterness. It becomes a way of life, and the work study profession is to blame! How many people in this country look upon work study as a top profession, and a good area in which to develop a career? The fact is that, properly controlled by management, work study standards are very high; and, if not controlled by management, they are very low.

Assessing how much Control Management has

If any manager of a company wishes to know if work study is well controlled, there are two simple ways to find out.

1   Look at the calculated performance levels in the company. If on average they are *above* 100–110, something is wrong.
2   Ask to see some element descriptions. Take the description, and compare it to the method being used by the operators. The detail involved in the description should be sufficient to reconstruct the method.

Where the method described is the one being used, then the times should be reasonable. Bear in mind that, if the description is very poor, such as 'Make up box', no one could possibly say that it was the same method. There are thousands of ways to make up a box!

Self-analysis by Management

Assuming the method is different, three questions should be asked of the departmental manager responsible.

1 Why did he not invite the work study department to change the standard time when the method changed?
2 If the element description is inadequate, why did he accept the time?
3 If he does not approve of the method in actual use, but does approve of the one in the element description, why is he allowing an unauthorised method to be used?

In most cases of loose times, the method will have changed, and the manager will not have invited work study to revise the time. Had there been a clearly defined policy of controlled work measurement, which the manager was responsible for carrying out, he clearly would be in error. Again, the normal truth of the situation is that it is not defined as a policy, and the manager could claim he was not fully aware of the implications. This situation is so widespread that one can only assume that managers at all levels simply do not realise how important this factor really is.

Hence, when one finds high performances, little or no method study, and constant quarrelling over how loose new times should be at the time of issue, management have failed to manage this particular part of the business!

Can one Regain Control?

For those companies that can recognise their own failing, there is still hope. The question that must be asked, however, is how can one begin to move towards a more controlled situation? How can the change be so structured that it will last for many years, perhaps even for the life of the company?

1 First admit that things could have been done better.
2 Consider very deeply how things can be restructured in

such a way that the standard time is no longer of such significance in calculating wages.

3　Prepare and discuss the possibility of a productivity agreement. This would include an evaluation of cost and benefit, and what proportion should be returned to the employees, and in which way.

Assuming a suitable formula could be found:

4　Establish a new incentive scheme structure, including a ceiling.
5　Provide for the employees a *continuing* means of seeking enhanced earnings through improved productivity.
6　Establish a sound policy of work measurement. This, of course, would include a clear identification of the role of the managers, plus ensuring that professional staff are employed at the right level.
7　Develop a programme of implementing new policies and systems.
8　Seek agreement, and implement programme.

The most important step, and the one on which it is predicted that many companies will stumble and fall, is the first one. To recognise after all those years that it was the fault of management, and not work study, is more than some people could cope with.

Next, company directors and senior executives must find a means to break the link between standard times and *excessive* earnings.

The major means of achieving this is shown in step 4 above, by gaining acceptance of a ceiling on bonus. There are two essential ingredients if it is still to be successful.

1　A sound policy on work measurement with management being aware of their responsibilities.
2　For preference, the incentive scheme should have some flexibility, with graded measured daywork being an excellent example.

To have a rigid ceiling would probably cause problems in the longer term. Equally any system of work measurement not properly managed will fail in the long term. If, therefore, any company decides upon a remeasurement programme, it must be logical not to repeat the same mistake all over again. As a simple guide, the bonus part of any wage should not add more than $33\frac{1}{3}$–50% to the basic wage. If the union wants more money, it should be negotiated onto the basic wage, or through other benefits. The idea that 'the higher the performance the lower the cost' must surely be better understood than it used to be. It is true in the short term, especially when introducing bonus, but it can move into reverse.

Management Commitment to Change

So a management commitment to change in policy may grow stronger. The next phase has to be thoroughly discussed and finally faced. The wages system is well embedded, and means must be found to *buy out* the old system, in order to regain the co-operation of the labour force. As explained in Chapter Three, the will to change is there, provided enough benefits can be seen by the employees. One factor that should be explored is the theories behind a high wage economy. There has never been a guarantee that low wages mean low costs, and it is not inevitable that high wages mean high costs. Improved productivity is the key; high wages, low costs, and full employment the prize. Naturally, the employees will want security of employment, hence the rate of change must be planned, gradual and controlled.

Many Alternative Systems

The possible variations on how this can be achieved are infinite. Changes are dependent upon particular company circumstances, the ingenuity of management, the benevolence of management, the wisdom of the unions, and the state of industrial relations at the time.

Several schemes that are known to have been implemented are described here as illustrations. They are not specifically recommended, but no doubt there are companies for whom either might work.

195

1 In one company a complete *rate audit* was agreed between management and the unions. This meant that everything had to be retimed, and new standard times issued. The new measurement programme was based on sound work measurement policy, and the new bonus scheme had a simple ceiling. The protection for the employees was that the old standard times were still retained, for employees there at the time of the agreement. For example, if a standard time of 3.00 SMs was found to be wrong by 1.00 SM, it was reissued as 2.00 SMs *plus* 1.00 XM (extra minute). All new members to the company were paid 2.00 SMs only, and existing members were paid 2.00 plus 1.00.

At first sight this may seem very unfair, but a blanket 10% was also put onto basic wages when the agreement was signed. All new employees had the position explained to them by personnel and a union member, and accepted the arrangement before a job was offered. Now clearly in this case the over-all effect of the change would take some years to be fulfilled. The immediate benefits were to the employees and were significant. Management would gain in time, as employees left, but without anyone really being hurt or dismayed by the change. The ceiling on performance was placed on SMs only, and XMs were used only for the calculation of extra bonus.

2 The second scheme worked with considerable success, but in some ways was more complex, and again concerned reductions in standard times. As a policy, it was agreed to move quite gradually towards a sound work measurement basis through a rate audit. Eventually, the object was to return to very soundly based SMs, carefully controlled by management, and by design of the incentive scheme. Again the secret for this scheme was the way in which benefits were shared with the employees.

As the standard times were 'corrected' a calculation was made as to how much the company would gain in the first instance, and an annual forecast of benefit was also made. Some of the cash saving was immediately given to the employees who lost the times, as in a suggestion scheme. A very significant amount was also paid into a carefully documented pool. Every time this pool reached 4% of the earnings of all company employees, wages were allowed to rise by 4%. Hence virtually all the direct savings made were returned to the employees. Some of this was on a personal basis, and some on a company-wide basis. The object here was to overcome any resistance that might be met from employees whose standard times were particularly loose, and thus stood to lose more by agreeing to the scheme. Administration staff can be included on the basis of non-replacement which causes a benefit to those remaining. As new jobs are introduced to the factory, they are put onto bonus fairly quickly. The ceiling prevents bonus earnings from rising too high, and the only way the employees can benefit is to have the standard times *reduced*. Hence, as they improve their methods and skills, and reach the limit of their bonus, but not a limit on output, they ask for a restudy. The lower the times are put, the greater the cash sum they receive, plus knowledge that some is going to the pool.

You may ask just exactly how does the company benefit? Well, for a start, there tends to be better industrial relations. Secondly, in many cases where times are not controlled, employees stop producing when they think their performance will cause an investigation, hence output is restricted. This system continuously encourages more output, as a 'true' 100 performance is always aimed for, and is always rising. Thirdly, there is a much wider acceptance of method study. If the employees cannot think up any further method improvements of their own, they may even ask if the work study department can help. Fourthly, the management have much more accurate planning and controlling, and pricing data. Finally, it reduces the gradual build-up of overmanning. In fact the concept of work study and standard times becomes more fun, instead of the basis of yet more grievances. It may not be perfect, but for some companies it would be far better than the non-controlled atmosphere they currently 'enjoy'. For the moment the type of schemes discussed above are really quite rare. Few people have experience in developing and negotiating a new approach.

The Benefits of a Revised System

Two possible schemes have been outlined for the company that already has realised the problems of poorly based incentive schemes. This point can be called *the point of disillusionment*. It is by no means a rare phenomenon; indeed many many companies have already reached this point. In fig. 77 there are three separate graphs. The first shows how productivity will continue to improve in most organisations which do not use incentives. This is due to changing technology, designs, and improved control. In general, the rate of improvement would be even greater, except for a fall in labour effort.

In the second graph, an incentive scheme causes labour effort to rise, and there are many advantages. Not only is labour used more effectively, but so are space, machines and other resources. The immediate impact, over the first three or four years, is quite noticeable. After a settling period, however, if the scheme was poorly based, the standard times that were so valuable begin to act as a barrier. As part of the 'wages contract', they became important to employees, who find the need to protect them. In effect they begin to slow down the normal rate of productivity improvement. After perhaps ten years or so, they are recognised by management as holding back the very improvement they were designed to bring. It is not unnatural for everyone to blame the system, and possibly spend even less and less money on its maintenance. This serves only to exacerbate the mistake they have already made. The mistake, of course, is *delegating* control of standard times to work study, without authority and allowing the times to become an important factor in wages maximisation. This is the type of company which *has to consider a change* in the system. A means should be found to return the company to its old path of productivity improvement. This is the ultimate purpose of this chapter. Such companies must consider how they can break the link between uncontrolled standard times and wages. It would be sheer folly to negotiate back to a position that seemed controlled, only for it immediately to start drifting again. A company that decides to move from an uncontrolled base must ensure that the alternative base is

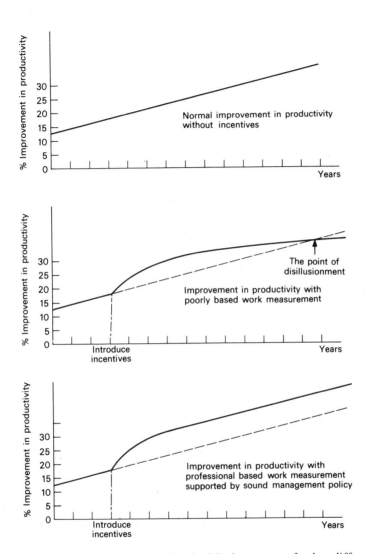

Fig. 77   Comparison of the rate of productivity improvement for three different companies.

controlled, otherwise it will not be worth the frustrations it will cause. See fig. 78.

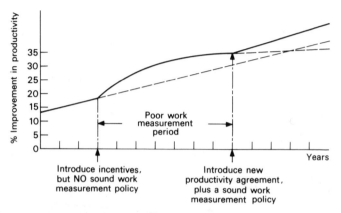

Fig. 78   How companies can return to productivity improvement and profit growth as an alternative to decline or closure.

In the third graph in fig. 77, the changes in productivity that would take place with the company that chose to have a controlled scheme right from the outset can be seen.

3   A third type of scheme that is quite well known is to buy out the old piecework scheme, or straight proportional, and replace it with measured daywork. This has been used in the car industry, and in the private sector of the steel industry. There has been limited success in both cases, but so much depends on the understanding of management. In one case, the major purpose of measured daywork was to put a limit on earnings, and take the pressure off the protective attitude of the employees towards their standard times. The buying out 'fee' was satisfactory for a few years, but then the old system began to look attractive to the employees once again. Probably the missing vital factor was the means of putting some of the benefits of improved productivity back into wages. In addition to this failure, the ceiling on bonus was single level, and rigid. Thus, in time, a new kind of problem began to occur, but for a different reason.

The Mistake of Control over Wages

It would be a mistake by management to negotiate a ceiling just to bring about control of wages. The people of this country still hope that the standard of living will slowly continue to rise. A control on wages helps to prevent this. Improving productivity, *and sharing the benefits*, allows standards of living to continue to rise. Obviously some of the benefit should go towards profit, some to future expansion, and some to keeping prices down.

4   Yet another company first introduced incentives about twenty years ago. After seven or eight years, it was found to be time to make a significant change. It was decided to start all over again. A complete remeasurement was proposed, but the employees, fearing loss of earnings, held a small strike. Pretty quickly, however, an agreement was reached. There were to be two schemes: the first a revised incentive scheme based on sound work measurement, and the second a company-wide productivity agreement. Many features were covered, and about two years taken to measure the whole factory. An interim payment was made during this time, and the management and unions met every week to discuss progress. Method study preceded most jobs before they were measured. As many different grades of pay had developed over the years, job evaluation was also agreed as part of the package. It was agreed that operators would learn more than one skill and accept flexibility.

During the implementation of the scheme, a learning allowance was made, dependent on the job.

Average performances after ten years are 110–120. Each time a new machine is introduced, the old standard times are left in until the end of the year, by agreement, and then the job is restudied and new times issued. Improvements due to improved productivity are calculated and a pool kept. Each time the figure reaches an agreed percentage of the wages bill, it is multiplied by a factor of say 0.5 to 0.7, and wages are increased by this percentage. The factor for reduction is related to how much of the change was due to the employees, and how much to technology and capital investment. The number of employees has grown significantly year by year: so has wages allowing for inflation, turnover, and of course the competitiveness of the company.

Here is yet another example of co-operation between employer and employees, to the benefit of everyone. The standard times were by no means the only change, but clearly played a central role. Job security, job satisfaction, and standard of living improvements are the benefits to the employees. It is a growth company, making sound profits, the benefit going to the employees in particular, and society in general.

Is there a Moral in this Book?

As, indeed *if*, more companies achieve this degree of co-operation, exports will grow, imports and unemployment will reduce, and the whole nation will win the ultimate prize. As a matter of interest, this would occur whether the nation was governed by a socialist or conservative party.

The moral of this book is one of co-operation. Instead of both management and unions feeling that work study and time study are something they must 'fight', they can develop a different view. That *new* view would be concerned with what *work study can do for people*. At the present time, many managements have become disillusioned with work study, and they feel that standard times and incentives are inhibiting. Members of the trade unions will want to protect the standard times they have, and wish to negotiate new ones. The unions inevitably see standard times as a means of improving wages, and after all is that not the way management designed the system of payment? If standard times, already issued and in daily use, allow high bonuses, how can they easily accept new ones that are more accurate? The work study professionals themselves are in many cases disillusioned with sitting in the middle. In endless cases they are encouraged to be less than professional by people who ought to know better. Maybe this is caused by employing a junior when a senior is needed. Maybe it is just asking for the job to be completed in a hurry, when it is more economic to do it more slowly. There are many cases of mere misjudgement, when companies decide to introduce incentives on the present methods. It is this decision that leads almost automatically to the point of disillusionment. The only likely variation from one company to another is how long it takes to reach that point and realise that it was a mistake. A major factor is management, who invite work study to issue times but then do not invite them to correct them when changes occur. Again it is believed that the increased output is reward enough, and the standard times *by implication* are accepted as permanent standards. Once again this is true, but only in the short term. Work study are given no authority at all to take additional studies when they feel they are needed. Unless they are invited back by management, they have no more control or responsibility over the times they prepared.

Are the Unions Really Happy with Poor Standards?

It would be too optimistic to surmise that the unions, at least, are happy with this situation. In the main they are not. They feel that they are protecting their members' interests, but in many cases this is not so. Ask the ex-employees of bankrupt companies. As the abuse of the standard time base leads inevitably to overmanning, once again there comes a time when the company is not only less competitive but noticeably so. How does the union proceed with wage negotiations then? They are thus less able to demand high wages and job security. If they do so, they will one day do this when the company is at its most vulnerable. As the company has always managed to find enough in the past, it will surely do so again. No doubt the company will have 'cried wolf' several times before they really needed to, and subsequently given in.

Overseas Competition – the New Factor

In the quite recent past, such situations have not been too critical. Competition now from overseas is becoming so intense that companies 'crying wolf' will be on the increase, and more and more will go bankrupt. These companies have probably had the problems referred to in this book for ten, twenty, perhaps even thirty years. Somehow, they have to wipe out the past and start again. This will only be done by working with the unions. If it is too one-sided, then the unions will feel forced to fight against their own wages providers instead of against the competitors.

Already, in Britain, many companies have closed, indeed whole industries are now non-existent. The products they used to make are still in demand, hence they must be imported. The typewriter industry is a fairly recent example. There are far too many obvious examples even to bother to name them. Our unions cannot be happy with this situation; certainly the employers are not. It would be wrong to try and point the finger of blame at either 'side'. The problem is not that one or the other is wrong, but that *both* are wrong, and both believe that it is the other 'side'. There are not two sides. We are all employees who work; we are all members of the same society. We all use the same roads, and the same services. In industry and commerce we should all create the wealth that we can then share equitably.

Co-operation

In Japan, it is known that there is a great deal of co-operation. Management and employees, engineers, work study, production planners and many others do work together, and very closely. The main object is to produce the goods, which produce the income. In the long run everyone gains.

A few companies in Britain have achieved the same degree of co-operation, and many more could benefit enormously if only they could find the secret. Part of this secret lies with the maintaining of standard times, and relating wage maximisation to improved productivity, not to improved labour performances based on obsolete times.

Remember that it is sales that pay wages, not times.

Index

Index of British Standard Terms